CHICKEN SOUP FOR THE
HORSE LOVER'S SOUL II

CHICKEN SOUP FOR THE HORSE LOVER'S SOUL II

Inspirational Tales of Passion, Achievement and Devotion

Jack Canfield, Mark Victor Hansen,
Marty Becker, D.V.M., Teresa Becker,
Peter Vegso and Theresa Peluso

Health Communications, Inc.
Deerfield Beach, Florida
www.hcibooks.com
www.chickensoup.com

We would like to acknowledge the many publishers and individuals who granted us permission to reprint the cited material. (Note: The stories that were written by Jack Canfield, Mark Victor Hansen, Marty Becker, Teresa Becker, Peter Vegso or Theresa Peluso are not included in this listing.)

The Heart of a Champion. Reprinted by permission of Alison Gieschen. ©2005 Alison Gieschen.

Abandoned Hay. Reprinted by permission of Kathleen Hooks. ©2004 Kathleen Hooks. Originally appeared in *Rocky Mountain Rider* magazine

The Wonder Pony. Reprinted by permission of Lauren Thoma. ©2005 Lauren Thoma.

Of Wind and Dreams. Reprinted by permission of Jane Middelton-Moz. ©2005 Jane Middelton-Moz.

B.J.'s Way. Reprinted by permission of Vikki Marshall. ©2005 Vikki Marshall.

Strips of Ribbon. Reprinted by permission of Sandra Newell. ©2005 Sandra Newell.

Side by Side, Together Again. Reprinted by permission of Sissy Burggraf. ©2005 Sissy Burggraf.

Compassion, Thy Name Is Anna. Reprinted by permission of Fred Glueckstein. ©2005 Fred Glueckstein.

Dawn Magic. Reprinted by permission of Lori Hein. ©2004 Lori Hein. Excerpted from *Ribbons of Highway: A Mother-Child Journey Across America.*

Found and Lost. Reprinted by permission of Tracy Van Buskirk. ©2003 Tracy Van Buskirk.

On Call. Reprinted by permission of Anne Hope. ©2002 Anne Hope.

(continued on page 268)

Library of Congress Cataloging-in-Publication Data
is on file with the Library of Congress.

© 2006 Jack Canfield and Mark Victor Hansen
ISBN 0-7573-0402-8

Publisher: Health Communications, Inc.
3201 S.W. 15th Street
Deerfield Beach, FL 33442-8190

Cover design by Larissa Hise Henoch
Inside formatting by Theresa Peluso and Dawn Von Strolley Grove

We dedicate this book to all horse lovers,
especially women, who nurture, protect and
love their equine companions so deeply.

Contents

1. ON COMPANIONSHIP AND COMMITMENT

2. HORSES AS TEACHERS

3. HORSES AS HEALERS

4. A SPECIAL BOND

5. JUST HORSIN' AROUND

Acknowledgments

Chicken Soup for the Horse Lover's Soul II is the culmination of a process that required the support and resilience of many people. Our families are a perpetual source of joy and love. Thank you, Inga, Christopher, Travis, Riley, Oran, Kyle, Patty, Elisabeth, Melanie, Mikkel, Lex, Anne, Melinda, Hayley and Brian.

The talented, enthusiastic staff, freelancers and interns who keep the wheels turning smoothly at Chicken Soup for the Soul Enterprises, Self-Esteem Seminars, Mark Victor Hansen and Associates, Pet Complex, and Health Communications are indispensable.

To help us select the best stories, we enlisted the help of a panel of volunteer readers who generously gave their time and shared their feedback. Our thanks and appreciation go out to Katherine Bontrager, Sissy Burggraf, Michelle Edwards, Corrine Everson, Leslie Henn, Barbara LoMonaco, Ann Magliaro, Donna Masterantonio, Kay McKinnie, Maryann Miller, Sue Miller, Karen Padgett, Marshall Rich, Jill Richardson, Betsy Sigmon, Diane Smith and Irene Wilkins.

And to everyone who submitted a story, we deeply appreciate your letting us into your lives. We regret that everyone's story could not be published, but we hope what was chosen for publication, which you are about to enjoy, conveys what was in your heart and in some way also tells your story.

Introduction

What is it about a horse that captures our hearts and minds?

Most of us can't remember a time when we didn't love horses. Some of us dreamed of horses before we ever saw one or we spoke of "horsey" shortly after, and sometimes before, the words "Momma" and "Dadda" came out of our mouths. We played with Breyer horses inside miniature corrals while friends were content to play with Barbies or Tonka toys. Were some of us just born with an inherent bond with these large and magnificent creatures, while others acquired the "horse bug" during infancy? In conversations and confessions with men and women from coast to coast, of every age, race and breed preference the collective answer in a shout is, "yes!"

Certainly, the love of horses goes much deeper than that of a typical hobby like gardening or golf. Being a horseperson isn't a lifestyle like that of folks who love exercise or the arts. Breed preference for a horse is much stronger than the partiality for a certain make or model of a pickup truck. Many women define their meeting of horses at a richer, deeper level, as nothing short of a calling in life. To some, the horse is a mirror into their innermost being, reflecting who they are and their purpose in life. To others, the horse is a connection to God, to the earth and to their spirituality.

We have found horses to be a conduit to becoming closer

to spouses, children, neighbors and friends by involving them in our equine activities. We learn many of life's lessons by groundwork with a horse as well as atop its strong back.

Many women speak of the nurturing instincts that a horse evokes in them. An animal that is so large, so strong, and at times so unpredictable, has come to rely on us to feed, care for, train and love it. We love the fact that they need us as much as we need them. Perhaps part of the magic is that this large and powerful animal responds to the gentlest of touches and gives back kindness and trust when treated with the same.

The companionship of a good horse is one of life's greatest joys. Being out on a mountain trail and experiencing its tranquil beauty, with the only sounds being the horse's breathing, hooves on the forest floor and the far-off gurgling of a clear, cold stream is therapy for the soul.

Time spent in the company of our horses takes much needed pressure off our other roles as a wife, husband, mother, father, friend and neighbor and makes us more human to other humans.

Those who compete in dressage, English, Western pleasure, rodeo or endurance know the "thrill of victory" and the "spills of defeat." Being in competition with a well-trained horse that responds to the subtlest of cues, and channels our expectations and dreams seemingly through thin air, is to be one with an animal. Whether you cry because you won a ribbon or because you have dirt in your eyes doesn't seem to really matter. Win or lose, you're a team. To one day say good-bye to a horse as it is humanely put to sleep in your arms is to know love, sadness, pain and reflection at the deepest level.

We invite you to enjoy what the writers in *Chicken Soup for the Horse Lover's Soul II* have to share. Their connection with horses allows us to not only laugh, cry and remember our own uniquely special experiences with horses, but to also celebrate the special bond each of us shares with our horses and which connects us to one another.

1

ON COMPANIONSHIP AND COMMITMENT

A horse gallops with his lungs,
Perseveres with his heart,
And wins with his character.

Tesio

The Heart of a Champion

Whether you think that you can, or that you can't, you are usually right.

Henry Ford

The powerful presence of our 2,000 pound draft horse, Janyck, belies a sweet disposition, which, along with his broad back, makes him the heart and soul of the vaulting team I coach. Vaulting is gymnastics on the back of a moving horse and our team is no less special than their horse. Janyck has changed the lives of the disadvantaged children he works with and they have come to love this horse. Abandonment, abuse, depression and anger are something these kids know all too well. Courage, strength, confidence and accomplishment are what Janyck introduced to their world. The events of one bitterly cold day in February 2002 would show his team and our entire community, just how special this horse really is.

It began with the shrill ring of the phone while we were getting ready for work and school. It was our neighbor across the road calling. Sometime in the early morning hours, Janyck had escaped from his stall and wandered over into their lake and fell through the ice. As we raced out of the house, three news helicopters and almost a hundred rescue workers had converged on the scene. The battle to rescue Janyck had begun. People from all over the area poured onto the farm to help in any way they could. One attempt after another failed to secure straps around our wet, frozen horse. Time ticked by with no success, each passing minute placing one more nail in our horse's coffin. The 16 degree temperature wreaked havoc with oil in the hydraulics on tow trucks and winches. Horse specialists where phoned for suggestions on how to attempt the rescue. As we huddled helplessly on the edge of the frozen pond, live coverage of the entire event was broadcast from circling helicopters. People jammed phone lines at the news stations, breaking records on the number of calls. They were late for work or called in sick and refused to leave the drama that was unfolding as they sat glued to their televisions waiting and hoping for a successful rescue.

Time and time again, Janyck was almost pulled to safety when the frozen straps would slip from his body and cast him back into the lake. Rescuers in bright red suits, contrasting against the white ice, brought out chainsaws to cut larger holes. One worker without a suit slipped and plunged into the frigid water next to the flailing horse and had to be rescued.

Two broken tow trucks and nearly three hours of agony later, our struggling half-frozen Janyck was finally dragged from the pond by a backhoe and the battle for his survival took a new turn; would he recover from being immersed in icy water for so long? This was no ordinary horse. He was the most important member of our team, and our children, their parents and their families were all depending on his survival. We dragged Janyck on a piece of plywood almost a quarter of a mile to an indoor arena that was part of the neighbor's farm. A large crowd circled around him. Construction workers from all over the local area showed up with space heaters. We pumped hot air onto him from every outlet in the arena while spasms racked his giant body as it tried to thaw and recirculate blood into his limbs.

My husband curled next to him desperately massaging his frozen legs, trying to get them working again. If a horse that size lies down for too long, his lungs begin to crush from his weight and he will die. Several times, he pulled all his strength together and attempted to stand, but he would wobble and crash face first into the dirt. His lips were bloody from crashing into the hard surface and each time he would fall, the entire group of onlookers would gasp and cry out in support.

I watched tearfully, feeling helpless, no more than a spectator, until I could watch no longer. "You get up, damn you, just get up now! I'm not going to lose you like this!" My horse and I have a very special connection and when he heard my voice, he lifted his head and made a giant effort to get to his feet. He struggled valiantly, failing again and again until finally, to the amazement of everyone, Janyck gave a tremendous push and steadied himself on giant, trembling legs. He stood, on shaking legs, but he stayed up. The crowd cheered and people grabbed one another, hugging and crying. I made it over to my husband and kissed him, then kissed my horse. No one would leave the scene until Janyck was on his feet.

Janyck was almost out of the woods. Hours after his rescue, covered in several blankets, his body still shivered. Waves of media showed up at the barn beaming live coverage on the noon, six and eleven o'clock news. At five the next morning, a news crew arrived to do a follow-up for *Good Day Philadelphia*. Exhausted, my husband and I listened as the anchor made a quick reference to local upcoming weather. We glanced at one another when he announced that a huge snowstorm was brewing in our area. Focused with concern for our horse, this was the first we had heard of the impending storm.

Two days later, four feet of snow blanketed our town. We had been making trips between our home and the barn preparing our little farm for the storm. My husband was plowing the driveway as the last of the storm was dumping its load of snow when my phone rang. The roof of a barn on our road with thirty horses in it had just collapsed due to the weight of the snow. There was only one barn on our road that fit the description and that was the barn with my recovering horse in it. The wail of police and fire engines filled the air as we raced toward the barn.

We could see the collapsed roof of the indoor arena where Janyck had regained the use of his legs and the partially collapsed roof pressing down on the stall area of the barn where we knew he would be. The frantic owner of the stable came running out of the barn with three horses in tow, yelling at us to get our horse out of the barn, now! Once again, we were racing against time and no one knew what horrible fate would follow if we lost this race. I started moving other horses to safety as my husband carefully extracted Janyck. Spooked by the screaming sirens of the emergency vehicles, Janyck bolted and dragged my husband for several hundred feet. He was unable to hold on as the powerful, scared animal raced away from the engines, directly toward the frozen lake. Some memory of what lay below must have surfaced because he stopped at the brink of the hill while my husband raced up to him and led him to the safety of our farm. Some of the neighbor's horses shared our small barn that snowy night, while others were shipped to nearby farms.

So began the second phase of our physical and emotional recovery. With hours of loving care from his teammates, Janyck regained his strength. In July, the American Vaulting Association hosted the 2004 National Vaulting Championships at the Lexington, Virginia, Horse Park. Janyck and the children who worked so hard on his recovery, and spent hours training and practicing in our very unique sport, joined hundreds of vaulters from around the country to compete for the top championships in their divisions. One of those vaulters was a twenty-year-old athlete from California, Blake Dahlgren. Blake would represent the United States in the World Equestrian Games in Stradl Paura, Austria, later in the month. Timing of the two events required Blake to ship his horse to Europe a month in advance of the World Championships and he had no horse to compete on at our own National event. When he arrived in Virginia, Blake walked around the various teams and spotted Janyck with his small, unknown team of vaulters practicing in earnest. Not knowing Janyck's story, he approached us, explained his dilemma and asked if he could try out our horse. Having a championship vaulter compete on Janyck was an honor and a thrill. Blake and Janyck spent a few days practicing before Blake defended his title on a new and unknown horse.

The final night of the competition arrived. Blake and another top competitor, who was able to compete on his own horse, tied for the championship. The last round of their individual Kur freestyle would be the tie breaker. Each man performed his one minute Kur routine and pulled out all the stops. They performed demanding routines that tested the incredible strength, flexibility and balance that this sport requires. The scores came in and the two men's performances were tied, equally. The tie breaker would come down to the score the horse received for his performance.

There are few horses that can balance themselves and carry a rider of Blake's weight and six-foot frame without wavering through a difficult routine. But Janyck's large heart, his amazing soul and his strength of will shone through once again. As the crowd waited in tense anticipation, the horse scores were announced. Janyck received a 7.8, the competitor's horse a 6.5. Janyck's horse score had won Blake the 2004 Men's Gold Championship title the day before he journeyed to the World Championships in Austria.

After Blake Dahlgren received his trophy and championship ribbon at the awards ceremony that night, he fought his way through the stands and found me. He pinned the championship ribbon on my shirt and simply said, "This is for Janyck. He deserves it."

Alison Gieschen

[AUTHOR'S NOTE: *Alison and her team competed at the 2005 National Championships in Denver, Colorado, and against all odds, the little team that could and the horse with the amazing heart were victorious and won the title of "C Team National Champions." They are only the second East Coast team in the thirty years of AVA nationals to win this title. The victory would not have been possible without Janyck and the patience he displayed as the girls practiced for up to six hours a day before the competition. The victory has only deepened their love and respect for this great animal.*]

Abandoned Hay

Every trial endured and weathered in the right spirit makes a soul nobler and stronger than it was before.

James Buckham

I started riding horses when I was seven. A decade later, I continued to devote my weekend mornings to cleaning stalls, feeding and turning out between eighteen and twenty-five horses for one important and enduring reason— I was always free to be my chronically awkward, occasionally angst-ridden and always raw, teenage self at the barn. Linna, my riding instructor, though the same age as my mom, taught me how to swear in unique, strangely cathartic and utterly tactless ways, instructed me in the fine art of cigarette smoking (thus eradicating my desire to ever touch another Marlboro again) and taught me how to ride. I found Linna when I was twelve and still couldn't figure out the correct diagonal or what it meant to "roll your hips forward."

A few lessons later, I was posting correctly and sticking my butt out while I trotted. Linna explained things so they made sense. She also helped my parents pay for part of my eleven-year-old horse, Rain Devil, and forever lamented that my track coach convinced me that my life's destiny was not to compete for the U.S. Olympic three-day team, but rather to break my high school's 800-meter record—neither of which I managed to accomplish.

Linna also kept Rain around for the first three years I was at Colgate University, which of course made the subsequent sale of my horse that much more piercing. By the time I left for college, Rain was suitable for lessons or leasing; she earned her own keep while I studied and ran my heart out for my college's track team seventy miles away. Rain was an ex-racehorse and retired broodmare when Linna brought her to Green Heron Farm. She was bony and ugly with awkward confirmation and was covered from head to toe with rain rot—skin fungus that I picked off diligently with my fingernails. Her feet were thrush-ridden, and she enjoyed rolling until she was entirely coated with a combination of crusty mud and other horses' manure. Rain felt like an unbalanced washing machine to ride and was known to destroy fences with her head rather than jump them during competitions. Rain and I had a love/hate relationship—we loved each other instantly, but no one could have guessed that from watching the two of us together.

Rain Devil, ears pinned tightly, bit me religiously when I'd tighten the girth and always kicked out threateningly when I'd nudge her forward with my outside leg. After a workout though, I'd feed her carrots and scratch the one spot under her neck that she'd tolerate me touching and she'd nuzzle my thigh after waiting patiently for me to remove her bridle. In horse language, she seemed to say, "Sorry, I was just kidding when I bit you before."

Rain, while a mare, reminded me of an immature boyfriend with whom you chronically play the game but who, in your own melodramatic, high-school state, are certain you love.

Then, when I was nineteen, I was diagnosed with multiple sclerosis and with the diagnosis, Rain grew up. She abandoned the game and found horse-type ways to feed me

carrots. I could no longer ride like I had before, yet something inside simultaneously demanded that I believe in God.
Weird, un-Rain-like things would happen. I'd ride her with
weakened legs and faltering balance and she'd slowly stop
just when I'd lose my right stirrup. I'd arrive at the barn
unable to traipse through the swamp-like, mud-infested
paddock and she'd sort of roll her eyes and saunter over to
me. She stopped biting my upper thigh when I adjusted the
saddle and no longer kicked-out when I asked her to canter.
When I left Colgate before the end of my junior year due to
a paralyzed right hand, Rain Devil was the only thing I
wanted to see.

I drove fifteen minutes from my house in Ithaca, New
York, to Linna's farm in Trumansburg and went directly to
the paddock that held Rain, the evening's hay supply and
enough mud to suck my tightly tied boots off of my feet. I
unlatched the gate knowing full well that I could go no further; I just stood there and watched her eat. And the whole
thing was so beautiful. My dark bay, fifteen-year-old horse
just standing there quietly eating her dinner, contemplating
which section of mud to roll around in next. Every once in a
while she'd glance in my direction and her eyes would say,
"Yes? What do you want?"

And there, in the mud, watching her chew, the numbness
of my hand transformed into the suffocating of my heart and
I started to cry. In between silent, snotty sobs, I started talking to her—just like I talked to her in high school when I was
in love with the wrong boys or angry with my mother.
Except this time, I said the same thing over and over again,
"Rain, I'm so scared right now, so scared." And then I'd cry
some more.

What happened next, though, was really the most divine
thing that ever happened to me at Green Heron Farm. Rain
Devil abandoned her pile of hay and walked over to me.
Before I could even move my desensitized fingers to her
mud-encrusted mane, she nuzzled her hay-filled muzzle to
my heart and left it there, barely pressing into me. Just

telling me that she loved me enough to stop eating and that she knew I was sad. So for a few minutes, the incessant fear and uncertainty about my future ceased and only a few things remained; a muddy horse, a pile of abandoned hay and more softness and beauty than my raw self had ever seen.

Kathleen Hooks

The Wonder Pony

*F*aith *is a knowledge within the heart, beyond the reach of proof.*

Kahlil Gibran

Nearly every little girl dreams at least once in her life of having her very own pony. One day it's going to be a pure white beautiful pony, so sweet it seems God himself made her out of sugar. Some times you'll have a jumping pony, a rich bay in color and you'll compete against the best of them. On another day, you're going to have a gleaming black pony. It will be a parade pony with braids in her mane and every little girl who's not lucky enough to have the pony will swoon at your privilege. But the best part of the dream is that she is your very own pony and the most precious thing in your life.

I imagine it must have been some early morning, and although the man at the meatpacking plant had had a long night, he was sure that the little yellow animal with a long white tail wasn't one of the steers that careened down the plank path. I can see him scratch his head as he considers the pony that calmly stands at the threshold of the semi-trailer full of beef on the hoof from South Dakota's grazing ranges.

Fortunately, the pony stays in the trailer until both levels of cattle unload themselves and stand lowing in the holding pen. The attendant approaches the pony and leads her off the truck by her furry white forelock and ties her to the bumper of his truck. Right now he has work to do, figuring out the future of a small yellow pony would have to wait.

"What?" Jean said after she answered the telephone at her stable. "Sure, they graze those steers in huge fields, anyone could have abandoned a pony by just tucking her in the gate one night." After a short pause I hear Jean continue, "Of course I'll take her, you can hardly wrap her up as a rump roast, can you?"

I sat on a hay bale writing my name in the dust on the stable wall. I was staying out of the barn aisle as my mom walked horses down to the indoor arena. I was only five years old at the time but I had loved horses for all of those five years, and I understood enough of the barn owner's one-sided conversation to hope that something very good was going to happen. I met my mom on her way back down the row of stalls and hopping from foot-to-foot I said, "I think a pony is coming! Jean said . . . and I heard her say . . . I think a pony is coming, Mom!" How right I was—a pony was coming.

Soon I had that wonderful dreamed of pony . . . well, maybe not all that wonderful, but she was mine! When we first met her, she was thin and filthy and her mane and tail were tangled and burr-ridden. She was too old for the vet to guess her age but she was just perfect to me. We spent many summer afternoons together, sometimes my mom would pony us down the road to an empty field and we would bring a picnic. Bailey would graze and we would snack and lie in the sun for awhile. The breeze would catch her white forelock and fluff it up into a white shrub between her tiny little cat-like ears.

Bailey was probably the most patient pony I have every met. In the winter we would put her little saddle on with her little breastplate and tie a Flexible Flier to the back with a lunge line. Someone would lead and someone would ride on the sled. We spent many happy hours in the snowy yard. Sometimes the sled would skid up against her furry little fetlock but Bailey didn't mind. I suspect she was glad to have a home in spite of its irregularities.

The wonder pony that Bailey was stayed with me as I shopped for a show horse when I was older, and I ended up with a lovely buckskin mare that I showed in Class A. We moved our horse family to a show barn full of lovely Arabian horses and, of course, Bailey came along too. Envision stall after stall of curvy necks and refined heads, shiny and slick over the top oak board, and right in the middle, two little yellow cat-like ears and a fluffy white forelock above two big brown eyes peering into the aisle waiting for the grain cart. Bailey was probably as out of place in the show barn as she was in the truck full of steers but everyone at the barn loved her.

The years have flown by since I sat in Jean's barn, writing on the wall with my wet finger, and Bailey has always been my pony. Other children would ride her around the arena at the stable. They would brush her long, thick mane and tail and say, "This is *my* pony," and, because I knew they were dreaming, I would smile and still know that Bailey would always be mine.

Bailey lived the life of a champion show horse in that barn. She wore a little blanket in the winter and was lovingly cared for, but even a champion show horse can't live forever. Bailey got sick and the vet came to see her every day. My little yellow pony had the best medicines and she stood in her deeply bedded stall with a fan in the door to keep her cool. She wouldn't eat and although she didn't seem to be in any pain, the light had left her eyes and she spent hour-after-hour lying in her stall. Finally one day Bailey got up and with determination knocked over the fan in the doorway, stepped over it and marched down the aisle past the lovely heads of her equine friends. Several of us in the barn followed Bailey outside. She seemed to be "on a mission" so nobody tried to grab her and interrupt her journey. Bailey walked briskly up the hill in front of the stable with her entourage of people trailing along behind. She walked to the old oak tree that stood outside the gate of the pasture she had always shared with the young foals that she babysat.

It was cool and breezy and Bailey lay down in the thick grass. I knew that it was time for her to go and I sat in the grass beside her. I lifted her head to my lap and smoothed her forelock down. I examined the way the fur on the dish of her face never laid straight and stroked the fuzz in her little cat-like ears. How I wished I could have been there for her birth, knew how old she was or even what breed she was. What would have happened if we hadn't taken her in? I wished I could have protected her at the time of her life where as far as the world knew, she didn't exist.

Soon her ribs rose less and less, her breathing slowed little by little and then stopped completely. I felt a tear stream down my face as the wind grabbed her smoothed forelock and fluffed it up again, as it had always been. I was grateful to have shared so many years with Bailey and to see her into God's hands. She was His now. She was finally home, where she really belonged.

Lauren Thoma

Of Wind and Dreams

*When you were born, you cried and the world
rejoice. Live your life in a manner so that when
you die the world cries and you rejoice.*

Native American Proverb

I could hear their whispers as we began cantering around
the rodeo grounds after our number was called, "I can't
believe she's riding that horse in this competition, look at
him!" "There's no way she can place on that animal, no way!"
As if in tandem, still echoing in my ears, were the words of
my guidance counselor the morning before, "There's no way
you'll get into that Eastern college you've got your heart set
on. No way! Your test scores just aren't high enough. Maybe
a secretarial school or a community college . . ."

Monte snorted as if he heard their collective voices in the
wind. Yet, as always, his head was up, proud as ever and so
was mine, hearing a stronger, unwavering voice. If the truth
were told, he wasn't the most beautiful horse in the world.
His huge workhorse body and thoroughbred legs made him
appear clumsy and out of proportion and, for my part, I certainly wasn't a top intellect in the left brain way of being. Yet,
Monte had learned a grace that could only have come from

sheer spirit and determination and, despite all predictions to the contrary, I was graduating with honors at the top of my class. So much of what we become is born on the backs of dreams or nightmares. Monte and I had dreams fueled by a fire there was no accounting for other than blind faith, a survival strength from birth that was kindled by those along the way who believed in us.

Monte was found by the river bank by my adopted uncle when he was a colt, barely alive, unwanted from birth. The same man befriended me when I was ten. He had given Monte to me and me to Monte. We were spirit mates, Monte and I, from the beginning.

The first place I had gone after hearing the guidance counselor's dire predictions was the ranch. Monte was far out in the pasture but heard the sound of my old Studebaker and was at the gate before I got out of my car. I met him at the gate, his halter in my hand, and tears streaming down my face. As on similar days in the past, clouded by the same predictions of my unworthiness, we rode hard and fast into the desert, leaving the echoes of voices behind, our spirits fueling each other, until the voices in the winds changed and belief returned.

Soon in the distance, I could see the familiar house of my adopted grandmother and grandfather, two elders who had given life to my spirit as if they had given me birth. The smile on the aged face of my grandfather assured me of my worthiness, "Look a bit down today, Sunshine. Looks like Monte brought you to the right place." His voice, as always, followed me on the ride home, "Remember, Sunshine, no one will ever hurt your spirit but you. You are in charge of your dreams. Without dreams and visions, we will be paralyzed never knowing on which path to place our feet. You and Monte make believers out of all of them tomorrow!"

"No way! No way!" The voices in the wind followed us as Monte galloped faster around the ring. My butt firmly in the saddle, my back straight, the reins held just right, we smoothly turned into the barrels. Western equitation had been as unfamiliar to Monte and me as five forks in a place setting in an upscale restaurant. Far from the bareback rides across the desert we had cherished over the years, it was a large part of the scoring and we had mastered the rules and were making believers out of the disbelievers in the crowd. Monte, now almost on his side, was racing around the barrels as gracefully as if he had wings touched by angels, not grazing even one barrel.

I glanced at the crowd as we cantered out of the ring and suddenly all I could see were the faces of my adopted aunts and uncles and the gentle nod from my adopted grandfather. "No one will hurt your spirit but you, Sunshine," echoed in the gentle wind that kissed my cheeks and my spirit, "No one!"

Before the judges called out our score, one came over and asked me to dismount. "We need to check for rosin on your saddle, little lady. It's hard to believe you could ride that huge animal, your rear never leaving the saddle, without some help, which you know is against the rules."

"No rosin, judge," I replied, "Check for yourself."

Monte and I tied for first place that day and he looked as proud as if he had run for the roses and won. I finished college and went on to graduate school, never learning until I was thirty that I was dyslexic—not just an "under-achiever," as I had been labeled. I finished writing my thirteenth book a month ago; copies of the first two were sent to my high school guidance counselor. Although Monte died when I was in graduate school, not a day goes by that I don't think of him and all those in my life that believed in both of us. In some strange way, I also often recall the gifts of those who didn't believe, who served to strengthen both my determination and the voices in the wind that have always gently guided me, challenged me and allowed me to follow my dreams.

Jane Middelton-Moz

B.J.'s Way

When you dig another out of their troubles, you find a place to bury your own.

Anonymous

Animals come into our lives to teach us important lessons. B.J. is one of those animals and when she dropped her big head into my chest, I knew the class had begun.

My big bay mare's official name is Barbizon's Jay and from her pedigree she turned out to be Thoroughbred royalty. I will always wonder why she was left to starve in a pasture after she had served her purpose. Horses need very little to survive—a bit of hay and water usually does the trick—but this was the first time I had looked into the eyes of a horse who had faced pure cruelty. That one look told me her story and it wasn't good.

B.J. carried the genetics of champions and the desire to run like the wind. Slapped with a racing saddle when she was a year and a half, B.J. was whipped into submission and taught to run faster than the herd behind her. She obliged but she tried so hard that injuries soon took her out of the game. A bowed tendon and a lacerated leg from a horse trailer accident left her scarred for life and no longer able to run. Her only defense was being a mare capable of birthing the future of Thoroughbred racing. What appeared an ideal existence, full of green pastures and other mares, became her downfall. B.J. was bred for ten consecutive years, producing foal after foal that surpassed her numbers in the game. All she asked for was food and water.

Being new to owning horses and apparently pretty naive when I first met B.J., I found myself coerced by a friend to go search for a horse with three criteria; cheap, pretty and stable enough for Civil War reenactment. On the agenda was a mare someone came across in a pasture that needed to be saved. What we saw was beyond imagination. Standing with great effort in the middle of a heat-ravaged field was a wound-laden bay mare. Her coat was littered with sores and not an ounce of shine, the vertebrae of her spine stood up better than she could. Her breathing was labored and she held her head down to the ground like a weak kickstand. My friend immediately turned around and left because although this mare was cheap, she was far from pretty. But I stayed put, mesmerized by what humans are capable of doing to animals. She looked at me with a sad black eye and tried to nicker but could not muster enough strength for the sound. As I moved closer, she managed to lift her head into my chest and rest it there as if she had found a home. She did.

It took months of careful nursing to bring B.J. back to life. While I wanted to stuff her full of grain and fresh alfalfa, her depleted stomach couldn't handle this simple indulgence at first. I bathed her and soothed her open wounds with dressings, hoping for a miracle, hoping to see something that resembled my other big and healthy Thoroughbreds that stood next to her in the barn. The hardest part was remembering to be quiet around her and to move with determination but absolutely no force, because it became obvious that she had suffered several harsh beatings by humans and the memories were as raw as her physical wounds. Slowly her eyes began to change. They softened and began to glow from within. Her nicker, once a whisper, now sang with the best of them and over time her weight and health were restored.

So I saved her. But the question was, now what was I going to do with her? I worked her gradually, deliberately and very, very quietly in a round pen just to see what she could do. She moved nice, but not perfectly, because of her old injuries. She hated loud noises and crowds so showing her was out of the question. She allowed me to ride her but snubbed away other hopefuls, and I soon realized I would not be able to part with this beautiful mare that finally trusted a human being to be kind. She became the lady of my barn, as sweet and unassuming an individual as I have ever encountered. Soon her bay coat shone dappled and healthy in the sunlight and if a horse could smile, I knew she would. Her life was no longer about her production; instead, her worth was just in being. She allowed me to see that simple acts of kindness give back in return. She taught me to enjoy the quiet and to look inward for strength but most important, she showed me how to survive through suffering.

My humble old mare is now twenty-eight and I've learned a thing or two about life and how it treats you. It isn't about where you came from, but who you're determined to be. B.J. has taught me this along with one of the hardest of human emotions . . . humility. As she ages gracefully, all she asks for is my care and in her everyday life she remains quietly modest, yet she still runs like the wind in her dreams—I've had the pleasure of seeing her do it during many of her contented catnaps.

Vikki Marshall

Strips of Ribbon

Courage does not always roar. Sometimes, it is the quiet voice at the end of the day saying, "I will try again tomorrow."

Anonymous

I lay alone in my king-size bed and couldn't stop the tears. *I'm just a stupid statistic,* I thought. *Thirty-one years old and getting divorced.* I had no idea how to get on with being this new "me"—single and alone—after nearly eleven years of being a "we." I had to stop torturing myself. After a quick shower and several layers of clothing, I was out the door and on my way to the ranch where I boarded my horse, a forty-five minute drive along the coast. There were just a few lone surfers battling the elements at Ocean Beach as I pulled over to Fredy's Deli for some fortification.

Fredy called out a good morning as he quickly prepared a sandwich and an obscenely large coffee with the works. If he noticed that my eyes were red rimmed from the earlier tears, he never said a word.

"You still want me to wrap half the sandwich?" he called out.

"Yeah, half for breakfast and half for dinner—it's the best deal in town," was my reply. And it really was. I was living on a limited budget and my horse, Kahluah, ate better than I did.

"So how is Kahluah doing?" asked Fredy as he handed me my order.

"Well, we've been working hard with Jo every week and I want to enter her in a local show that's coming up, but Jo and well everyone, is going out of town, so . . ." I trailed off and took a big swig of coffee.

"Why can't you go to the show by yourself?" Fredy the non-horseperson asked.

"There's all kinds of reasons, Fredy, but mostly it would be really hard to sign up, get my number, warm up—you know a million things could go wrong and I really could use a hand and . . ."

"You don't have a trailer." Fredy finished my sentence for me.

"Actually, this show is right next door to our ranch. I could just ride over, I mean if I was going to show at all. Which I am not."

Fredy came out from behind the counter and began restocking the napkins.

"You know, it seems to me that when you first started coming in here all you could do was talk about that horse and how you rescued her and all. You couldn't wait for her to get healthy and fit so you could take her to a horse show. It was always 'Kahluah did this and Kahluah did that.' Now you got a chance to show her and you don't want to? I don't understand." Fredy shook his head.

I had a hard time understanding myself. When I came across an ad for an eleven-year-old Trakehner mare advertised for only $1000, I couldn't believe that a Trakehner would be so cheap. "You get what you pay for," immediately came to mind as I drove several hours to see my dream horse.

What I got was an emaciated, worm-infested, dark bay, Trakehner mare. She was sick and lifeless. I took one look into her huge brown eyes and brought her home. It was that simple. I never stopped to think about why I was taking on such a huge, time-consuming project. I never questioned where I was going to get the extra money it would take to nurse her back to health. All I knew was that I instantly loved this horse and she needed me. I would do whatever it took to see life glowing in her again. I was bringing her home.

Home was a large boarding facility on the San Mateo coast. When she walked off that trailer, my vet gave her twenty-four hours to live. If she did live, he said I was in for a lot of work. She had to be wormed slowly and fed just as judiciously. In the beginning, she had only enough energy to eat. I brushed her thin body for hours and talked to her about all that was happening in my life. I traced my hands over her ribs and vertebrae, silently wondering if she would ever be able to trust in me to do right by her. Her dread-locked mane and tail were combed out and she grew in a winter coat to battle the coastal chill.

I lived for her soft nickers.

Life evolved into a whole new routine that winter. My husband, Bryan, started to work the graveyard shift and our relationship was made up of notes and the occasional phone call. It was the beginning of the end. I tried to ignore the gnawing feeling that my marriage was in trouble and spent more and more time with Kahluah.

I made new friends at the ranch and we jokingly called ourselves "the night crew," as darkness fell earlier and earlier. Kahluah blossomed under all the love and attention. I was in no hurry to get home to an empty apartment, so I devoted all my time to this wonderful creature in my life. I poured out my frustrations with my job and clipped a bridle path. I lamented that I never saw my husband and banged her tail. Then the winter rain came along with the need for flashlights and propane lamps. Kahluah seemed content to share her grain bucket while I drank hot chocolate from a thermos. Her body heat warmed us both as we shared her run-in and listened to the rain fall. I realized that for the first time in a long time I felt fulfilled even as my marriage was crumbling around me. The smell of the shavings and the sounds of her munching were therapy for my soul. I wondered who had rescued who on my long dark drives back into the city.

Now two years later, Kahluah was sound and fit. Her dark brown coat shone with a million strokes. She had filled out and my skinny, stick mare was no longer. I estimated that she had put on over 250 pounds. I had a whopping 16.1-hand energetic ball of fire. The lovely Trakehner floating trot was evident in her joyful laps around the arena. She snorted, squealed and blew huge breaths in her summer delight. We started training with a local trainer and I was thrilled in her responses. Kahluah was eager to please and was patient with my rusty aids. Our formal lessons were broken up with bareback trail rides up and down the coastal hills. She imparted such freedom, I never felt more alive than when we were galloping across the black soil of the farmer's fields with the ocean sun casting our shadows like winged souls. I trusted her implicitly.

Fredy interrupted my reverie. "You know, Sam, I know you've been through a hard time with the whole divorce and all, but you can't let the sadness inside you ruin everything in your life."

I was shocked. Fredy had never spoken to me directly about my divorce. Our small talk had always been on safe ground. A customer banged into the deli and I was saved.

"Bye, Fredy. Thanks." I bolted out of the door and into the safety of my truck.

The miles flashed by and my anger and sadness began to build. I felt so alone, so much like a loser for failing to keep my marriage together. But then I began to realize that perhaps Kahluah, in some instinctive way, had felt alone as well. She needed me and right now I needed her. Was I going to let one mistake suck all of the joy out of my life? And, as I pulled into the dirt driveway of the ranch, my partner stuck her head out of her run-in and whinnied. I guess I had my answer—I was going to show.

The day of the show I was up at 0'dark-hundred and was thankful for clear weather. Riding over to the neighboring ranch, I filled my mind with the sounds, smells and emotions that I experienced when riding as one with Kahluah. I heard the softest creak of leather, I smelled the salt air and I felt my heart grow lighter. I sat deeper, remembered to breathe and relaxed my body. Suddenly I was hungry for a taste of winning. I remembered that I had some talent, but more important, I had faith in my mare and myself. We were a winning combination and I wanted to prove it.

After tying Kahluah up, I signed up for my classes and had my number pinned on by the harried steward. I was able to find a spot on the rail in the warm-up arena and felt my horse move beneath me. I breathed in and out slowly and asked for simple changes in pace. Kahluah responded effortlessly.

The announcer called for the first class and we moved toward the huge arena. It was a Hunter under Saddle equitation class with fifteen riders. I saw only the space between my mare's pricked ears as the judge called out for a working trot. I concentrated on my mare's rhythmic breaths and before I knew it, the judging was over and the class was asked to line up. When the announcer called us out of the line up for the blue, I hesitated for just a tiny fraction. It was the last time I hesitated that day.

By day's end, we had taken three firsts and two second place ribbons. We were on fire. The tightness in my chest came from the pride I felt. I wanted the whole world to see what a wondrous creature had ascended to take this show by storm. All too soon, the day was done.

I hand-walked Kahluah home and put her up for the night. She munched her grain bucket and nudged me for more scratches on her back. She was relaxed and peaceful and I was exhausted. The ranch was deserted except for the lone barn cat slumming down our way. It was time to go home.

As I drove along Highway One and entered the city

limits, I waited for the familiar dread to invade my thoughts, but it never came. Instead, I looked down at the strips of blue and red ribbon lying on my truck's seat and laughed out loud. I couldn't wait to see Fredy the next day and show him my bounty.

Sandra Newell

Side by Side, Together Again

Old friends pass away, new friends appear. It is just like the days. An old day passes, a new day arrives. The important thing is to make it meaningful: a meaningful friend—or a meaningful day.

Dalai Lama

Dee and Rosie were inseparable. They were aged mares kept in the same stall for twenty-eight years, enduring one of the worst cases of neglect I can recall. Fourteen months after she and Dee arrived at my rescue and rehabilitation center in Chillicothe, Ohio, Rosie passed on. While they lived with us, Dee and Rosie were well cared for and loved. They learned to be horses again and experienced simple things, like the touch of grass under their hooves—something they hadn't felt since they were six months old.

For two years following Rosie's death, Dee was a loner. Whether it was her grief or her dedication to Rosie, I don't know. Perhaps she still saw Rosie by her side, but she didn't seem to need, or want, the company of other horses. Until Brandy.

Brandy came to us with a severe heart condition and did

well for the first few years she was here. Inevitably, age took its toll and with it came deafness for Brandy. Curiously, Brandy's affliction seemed to revive Dee's desire for a companion to care for. She and another horse, Dena, became Brandy's guardian angels—as well as her ears. Dee and Dena never left Brandy's side and when someone, or something, happened by they made sure Brandy was well aware of it and the first to move to safety.

The girls, as we knew them, continued their guardian duties for the next couple of years. I marveled at how they cared for each other; always devoted, always there for one another. As I watched them in the field one day, I noticed that Brandy was suddenly somehow "different," appearing weak and somewhat disoriented. Dee and Dena gathered closer as Brandy lay down at their feet. With her angels by her side, Brandy quietly and quickly passed away at the age of forty-three from a heart attack. I covered Brandy until we could bury her later that day, but the girls remained with her the entire time. In death, as in life, they would protect her.

Horses, like humans, must grieve in their own ways, in their own time. Dee and Dena remained together, until at the age of forty-one, Dena was humanely euthanized when a stroke left her paralyzed from the neck down. Dee was a faithful, compassionate caretaker and guardian angel for every one of her companions, but I know none could ever take Rosie's place in her heart.

The winter of 2004 would come and go with snow, ice and bone-chilling cold. One night while feeding, I noticed an additional horse in the field. It was standing at a distance and, with the darkness, it was difficult to be certain exactly which horse it was. Two things were certain. It was a black horse, either Raven or Dena, and both of these horses had passed away a year or more ago.

I went into the house to tell my husband what I had witnessed in the field. I had been surprised, but not afraid, and the more I thought about it, I had the feeling it was Dena.

My husband had recently returned home from the hospital after open heart surgery and I felt Dena was back at her angel duties, here to reassure me that everything would be okay. Dena appeared in the field for two more nights.

The spring rains had begun so each evening I led Dee and the other horses into the barn to spend the night warm and dry. On the third evening, the girls willingly went into their stalls, except Dee. After what seemed like hours of bribing and coaxing, Dee reluctantly followed me into her stall after I assured her I would turn her out first thing in the morning. I told the three girls goodnight, turned out the lights and left the barn.

The first thing the following morning I went to the barn as promised. I opened Gina's stall but she didn't go out. I noticed that Shasha was standing with her head over the stall wall, looking into Dee's stall. I didn't see Dee's head and hoped against hope that she just had her head down eating. I opened Shasha's stall and she, too, only stood there.

I walked to Dee's stall. My blood ran cold, my breath caught and the tears fell as I looked in at her lifeless forty-year-old body. My beloved Dee, my guardian angel of all, who had spent twenty-eight years of her life imprisoned in a barn, had now spent her last night on earth in one—against her wants and wishes.

It was so much clearer now; why Dee had fussed about going into her stall, why Dena had been in the field the two nights before and again last night when Dee resisted coming in out of the rain. I now understood that Dee had no plans of standing in the rain, but meant to join Dena so together they could cross the Rainbow Bridge to be reunited with her beloved Rosie once again.

We buried Dee that evening in the glow of the sunset, beneath a dogwood tree in full bloom. As I knelt down next to her to say my final good-byes, the dogwood petals began to fall. Softly, one by one, they fell on Dee's face and her beautiful chestnut body. With each petal, it seemed as if my darling Dee was telling me to dry my tears, that she and

Rosie were—at last—safe, happy and together once again.

I go to Dee's grave every evening, to be sure it stays safe and secure, and to tell her how much I still love her. As I make my way out to my favorite spot under the dogwood tree, I always find myself searching the quiet fields, searching in hopes of seeing my two old girls, Dee and Rosie, side by side, together again.

Sissy Burggraf

Compassion, Thy Name Is Anna

I have been writing a little book, its special aim being to induce kindness, sympathy and an understanding treatment of horses.

From Anna Sewell's Diary

While growing up in nineteenth century Victorian England, Anna Sewell often saw people abusing their horses in the city and countryside. Horses were brutally whipped, underfed and asked to cart loads that were much too heavy. These animals worked in sweltering heat, freezing cold, driving rain and heavy snow—often seven days a week, year after year—until they died from exhaustion. As a devout Quaker, such abuse was extremely distressing to Anna. These injustices left her with a lifelong fervor to right the wrongs done to those powerless and noble animals she loved so dearly.

It began with a dream: to persuade adults to treat horses with sympathy and compassion. To try and accomplish her desire, Anna decided to write a "little book." *Black Beauty*— the only book she ever wrote—was conceived as fictional autobiography of a gentle and well-bred horse. Written as a powerful moral tale, *Black Beauty* became one of the most popular and best-loved children's classics in the English language.

The mistreatment of horses in England was perhaps best symbolized by the bearing rein, also known as a checkrein in the United States. Used on horse-drawn carriages and carts, the bearing rein was connected from the animal's bit to the harness. It kept a horse's head high and gave the neck an unnatural graceful curve, having no purpose other than to improve the fashionable appearance of the animal. Horses forced to use the bearing rein suffered serious respiratory problems, reduced vision and loss of balance, which often resulted in pain, illness and death.

Anna hated the bearing rein and wanted the practice ended. Often Anna's outrage and fiery temper led her to confront full-grown men from all walks of life and to admonish them on the use of the bearing rein. The reason for acting on such injustices was perhaps best articulated by one of her characters in *Black Beauty*—a gentleman who intervened when he saw a carter brutally punish his horses with a whip and rein. "My doctrine is this," said the gentleman to his friend, "that if we see cruelty or wrong that we have the power to stop and do nothing, we make ourselves sharers in the guilt."

Anna Sewell was born March 30, 1820, in the seaside town of Great Yarmouth, Norfolk, England, to strict Quaker parents who used the biblical forms of "thee" and "thou." Her mother, Mary, taught Anna and brother, Philip, the virtues of honesty, industry, thrift, self-reliance and self-denial. She also instilled in them qualities she practiced, self-sacrifice and helping the poor. Anna and Philip were also taught to be kind to animals, an important article of the Quaker code.

Anna was a pretty child with dark curly hair. At an early age, she showed artistic talent and a gift for languages. At the age of fourteen, she had an accident, which changed her life forever. Coming home from school one day, Anna was caught in a heavy rain storm without an umbrella. While running up the sloping carriage drive leading to her house, she fell, twisting her ankles so badly, she could not stand.

Anna's ankles never healed. For the rest of her life, she was a semi-invalid, who never married and lived at home. By 1845, Anna's health deteriorated and she had more difficulty walking. Forced to drive a pony and chaise to get around, she soon learned to understand the nature and habits of her horse.

At the age of fifty-one, Anna was struck by a disease, the exact nature of which has never been determined. Poor health confined her to her home where she rested on the sofa most of the day. An entry in her diary for November 6, 1871, showed she had begun *Black Beauty*. She wrote: "I am writing the life of a horse and getting dolls and boxes ready for Christmas." Over the next five years, except from time-to-time when a few portions were dictated to her mother, Anna's poor health did not allow her to read or write. When Anna's health improved somewhat, she wrote more often. Mary afterwards took her writing and copied it. At other times, when Anna was not well enough to write, she told her tale to her mother, who wrote it down.

With her mother's encouragement, Anna completed *Black Beauty* in 1877. The book was the story of a gentle black horse with one white foot and a white star on his forehead that told his own story from youth to old age. By writing *Black Beauty* as a horse's autobiography, Anna wanted the reader to hear about the joys and sorrows of Black Beauty and his friends—Ginger, Merrylegs, Justice, Sir Oliver and Captain—in their own words. The plea for understanding and compassion came from the animals.

Foremost, Anna wrote *Black Beauty* as a primer on what to do and what not to do in caring for a horse. However, its charm and appeal was the story. *Black Beauty* opened with the horse recalling his early home, a place of tranquility and comfort. Black Beauty was sold at four years of age, beginning a life's journey of good and bad times that depended on the temperament of his owner.

Anna wrote of good and caring people such as the master,

the Squire and Mrs. Gordon of Birtwick Park, the coachman John Manley and stable boy James Howard. She also wrote about Black Beauty's cruel owners, who because of ignorance, ill temper, alcohol or neglect caused Black Beauty pain, serious injury or near death.

Capturing the imagination of children and adults for generations, Anna presented many dramatic and unforgettable scenes. There was the excitement of the moonlight gallop to fetch the doctor for the Squire's wife, the story of the flooded bridge, the fire in the stables at the coach's inn and the sad and tragic encounter years later between Black Beauty and Ginger as lowly cab horses in the drab streets of London.

Anna Sewell's death came five months after the publication of *Black Beauty*. After a long night of painful breathing and incessant coughing, a nurse called Mary and Philip to Anna's bedside in the early morning hours of April 25, 1878. When the end was near, Philip offered final prayers.

On the day of Anna's burial in the family plot at Lammas in Norfolk, Mary Sewell looked out of the window of the upstairs drawing room as the horse-drawn funeral hearse drew up to the door. Her friend and neighbor Mrs. Buxton was present. Appalled by what she saw, Mrs. Sewell exclaimed, "Oh this will never do!" and ran down the stairs and out of the house, ordering the carriage driver to remove the bearing reins from all the horses in the cortege. Anna's beloved animals would never again suffer the widespread abuse and pain she had witnessed in her lifetime.

Fred Glueckstein

Dawn Magic

Most people live and die with their music still unplayed. They never dare to try.

Mary Kay Ash

A bridge over the Big Sandy River took us over the state line. Dusty, ochre ugliness. Kentucky wasn't supposed to be dry and beige. It was supposed to be rich and green. What was this brown limestone world, this claylike landscape of dirty yellow rock, this Daniel Boone Forest that didn't seem to have any trees? I made an emergency stop at the Ponderosa buffet in Morehead, so we could fill ourselves with comfort food and recover from the disappointment of learning that Kentucky—at least this part of it—was not very pretty.

Closer to Lexington, redemption. Hints of green and blue. Patches, then whole pastures, of rolling, perfect grass. Grass that nurtures champions. Mare and foal pairs in love and nuzzling, savoring their time together, sunlight on their withers. Horses so beautiful you want to cry. Elegance and long legs and strong backs and power bred for a purpose. This was Lexington.

My daughter Dana's dream became real, mile by white

rail-fenced mile. The horses were pure majesty. I watched my son, Adam, watch Dana. I could see him decide to go with the flow and let his sister enjoy. I filled up. My daughter was in her place of a young lifetime, we were surrounded by equine beauty that took your breath away and Adam was showing himself to be a true gentleman.

Our Lexington days were all horse. We made an eight-hour, 85-degree-in-the-shade, no-square-inch-missed visit to Kentucky Horse Park. We went three times to Thoroughbred Park to leap among and sit atop the life-size bronze Derby contenders. We stalked a pair of Lexington cops and their chestnut mounts as they walked their Main Street beat. "The police even ride horses!" marveled Dana, as she added law enforcement to her mental list of jobs for horse lovers.

I don't think Dana slept much the night before our dawn pilgrimage to Keeneland Racecourse to watch the morning workouts. When I whispered in her ear at 5:30 that it was time to get up, her eyes shot open and her face beamed. We dressed quietly so we wouldn't wake Adam, slipped out and went downstairs for a quick breakfast before heading into the already hot Lexington pre-dawn. We were the first breakfast customers of the morning. As we passed the reception desk, I whispered to the clerk, "We're off to Keeneland." "Ahhhh," she whispered back, nodding at Dana with a knowing look, telepathy transmitted from one horse lover to another. "You'll love it." I looked at Dana, always beautiful and, at this moment, the most excited, gorgeous little girl on the planet.

We traced a route around venerable Keeneland along parts of the Bluegrass Driving Tour, following Rice and Van Meter and Versailles. "We say 'ver-SALES,' not fancy like the one in France," the night desk clerk had told me when I'd come down to ask the best route from the hotel to Keeneland. Dana could have spent hours on these roads, each a thin, gray ribbon along which lay some of Lexington's most storied horse farms. The pastures were lush green carpet, the architecture distinctive and utterly beautiful. Crisp lines, fresh paint, rich trim. Pristine clapboards and elegant cupolas, graceful weathervanes.

Dana has an encyclopedic knowledge of everything equine and, from her reading, was more familiar with these farms than I. Her excitement as we read their names—John Ward, Drumkenny, Broodmare, Manchester, Fares—traveled like an electrical current, stirring in me a deep contentment. We pulled over by a white rail fence on a slight rise in Rice Boulevard and looked out over the pastures spreading before us, hints of blue visible in the rich grass as it waited in the low, early light for the new day to burn off the night's dew and mist.

On Van Meter, the red trim on the outbuildings of a vast farm betrayed it as Calumet and, as we neared its fences, from a stand of tall trees that graced a velvety grass hillock, came a line of grooms, all Latino, each man leading a stunning Thoroughbred on a rope. The line of small, silent men and sinewy horses flowed down the hillock toward us, then turned left and continued, parallel to the fence and the road we watched from, keeping under the shade of the trees, then turned left again, gently ambling back up the rise toward Calumet's stables.

At Keeneland, we stood at the rail of the fabled oval, the only spectators, and watched trainers lead horses from the misty rows of silvery stables and onto the track. Light, lean, blue-jeaned trainers, one with dreadlocks flying from under his helmet, put pounding, sweating Thoroughbreds through their paces. The trainers wore helmets and most wore chest pads. They carried crops, which they weren't shy about using. Some stood, others crouched. Some made their horses step sideways. The men and animals took the track's bends and straightaways at breakneck speeds. Old Joe, tall and gaunt and wrinkled, in jeans and western shirt and a helmet with a pom-pom on top, sat astride his horse, Frog. They sat at the track rail, inside and on the course, ready to go after runaways. That was their job. Joe's eyes were peeled and he was ready to ride Frog to the rescue of any trainer whose trainee decided he'd rather be somewhere else.

A good number of the riders took note of Dana. A little girl with a beautiful brown ponytail who'd risen before the sun to stand at the rail. Like this morning's desk clerk, they recognized her as a kindred spirit. They smiled, waved and slowed down when they passed so she could look longer at their horses. Dana had brought her little plastic camera and some of the trainers posed for pictures.

One trainer with a gentle face and shining eyes assembled himself and three others into a parade formation. They passed us, four abreast, at a slow, regal posting trot, like palace guard presenting the colors before the queen, each rider smiling down at Dana. I thanked them with my eyes. That they took note and took time turned this special morning into magic. These were busy men with hard work to do. Some were watched by the horse owners who paid them and they weren't paid to be nice to little girls. But they were and I'll always remember them with fondness.

Before we left Keeneland, as the first brush of hot, higher-than-horizon sun kissed the bluegrass, we ventured into the great grandstand and sat awhile in "Mr. George Goodman's" personalized box, imagining what it would be like to settle in here in the cool shade on a sunny race day to watch the horses and the other race goers.

Adam had slept until we turned the key back in the door. "Breakfast is about to close. You'd better get down there, bud." On this trip, I left no hotel amenity unturned, amassing a sack full of little soaps and bottles of shampoo that I used to wash our clothes in the sink or bathtub. And, I encouraged the eating of any available free food. I looked for the magic words "Free Continental Breakfast" on motel signs. Sometimes we hit pay dirt, finding a motel that also hosted a "Manager's Happy Hour." This meant free dinner, because, next to the beer and wine and soda, the manager usually laid out cheese and crackers and a big tray of crudités. The kids drew the line at raw cauliflower and broccoli, but tucked into the celery, carrots and cherry tomatoes, huge dollops of dip on the side. Sometimes pay dirt turned to mother lode, with a spread that included things like tacos and little egg rolls.

Through careful husbandry of free motel fare and a manager's cocktail hour here and there, we were occasionally able to patch together a string of five free meals in a row. By meal number six, we were ready for a restaurant and we always voted unanimously on type: Mexican.

Dana and I accompanied Adam down to the breakfast bar. "So, how was it?" he asked, of our visit to Keeneland. He asked Dana, directly. I wanted to hug him over his plate of biscuits and gravy. As she wove a tale of the magic kingdom of Keeneland, Adam listened and chewed. While it was clear he thought Keeneland sounded cool—he said "okay" a few times as Dana talked—I knew he didn't feel he'd missed anything. Dana preferred horses, he preferred sleep. He was content they'd both gotten what they most wanted from the morning.

That night, while I worked on my first installment for the newspaper, Dana was writing her own story, "Horse Capital of the World." It begins: "In the heart of Lexington, Kentucky, lies a beauty like no other . . .

Lori Hein

Found and Lost

Remember where you have been and know where you are going. Life is not a race, but a journey to be savored each step of the way.

Nikita Koloff

"He's in that stall over there." The wrangler waved his dirty white cowboy hat toward the box stall at the end of the barn. I walked over and took a look. Dark equine eyes stared back with interest. "He was bred on an Arabian ranch in Wyoming. Ran free for a year. Halter-broke, gelded and released. He's barely had a human hand on him in three years. He was roped, loaded on a trailer and brought here to sell. Heard he put up quite a fight."

I was at a stable on the outskirts of Denver and at twenty-two, was trying to figure out what to do with my life by running away from it. I was two months into what was to become a year-long, cross-country trek in a big Chevy pickup truck pulling a rusty stock trailer. My simple plan was to get a horse and travel.

I took a closer look at the horse in the stall. His ears were too long and his head too big for a classic Arabian. But his dark, gun-metal gray coat was velvety, save for the vicious rope burns around his neck. For all the apparent trauma he had been through, he regarded me calmly and did not shy away from my hand. The cowboy in the white hat led him out to a small corral. I clucked to get him moving. Head up, tail up, in the indomitable Arabian style, he simply floated around the ring. I had never seen a horse move so smoothly and effortlessly. There was no question. He became mine. He took well to bridle and saddle, but there was a wildness to him that simmered just below the surface. I named him Colorado and he joined me on my adventure.

The rest of the summer and fall was a true vagabond existence. I had no goals, no schedule, no plans and I loved it. I wandered farther out West, to Wyoming and Montana, sometimes traveling with friends, sometimes alone. Nights were spent camping in a tent, with Colorado tied nearby. I felt totally content as I drifted to sleep to the sound of stamping hooves and the smell of horse sweat and hay. I would park the truck and take my horse high into the mountains for days on end. One morning I woke up before dawn, slipped out of the tent, climbed bareback onto Colorado and let him lead me deep into the aspens. We stopped by a stream and while we were standing quietly, I watched a buck with magnificent antlers slip down near us to drink for a moment.

But despite my efforts to avoid it, responsibility tracked me down. The need for a job led me back east. I somehow secured a job at an international bank. I rented a small house for me and a field in the country for Colorado. My life quickly filled with conservative blazers, memos, calls to London and the newspaper each morning on the train. I struggled through each week and lived for the weekend. On Saturday mornings, I pulled on my oldest jeans and scuffed boots and headed up to the country. Colorado had easily ensconced himself as the lead horse in a motley herd of a dozen complacent riding horses. The wildness of his past was manifested in his cheerful refusal to be caught, which could only be overcome with patience, subterfuge and a bucket of grain. I would pull the burrs out of his mane, inhale his sweaty sweetness and we would ride into the woods. My current life would slough off and I would forget that I chafed at my job, had little in common with my current boyfriend and that I missed my past adventures terribly. Instead, I simply enjoyed the feel of my horse under me. My past wildness, like that of Colorado's, would return. Colorado loved to run and my heart filled with true joy as we galloped across wet fields with his mane slapping at my hands. He was my soul mate.

Eventually the boyfriend disappeared from my life and I met a young ex-photographer's assistant on the train and fell in love. We married soon after, bought a house and my conformity with the rest of the world increased. Sometimes I couldn't believe how different my life had become since my vagabond days. But I still had Colorado. Age had lightened his dark gray coat to cloudy silver. He still waited for me in his field each weekend, playfully dodging my rope as I walked closer. Then, with ears and tail up, galloped me effortlessly back into the freedom of my past.

It had been ten years since I first saw Colorado in that barn in Denver. My job responsibilities had grown and I was now comfortable in my business suit and with office politics. My husband had morphed into a successful engineer at a big company. Some weekends I didn't make it out to Colorado's field for a ride and a swell of guilt would pass through me on a Saturday morning when I found myself working on the house or shopping at the mall. A baby girl was born and before I knew it, a boy followed. Sometimes, I would drive by Colorado's field with the children strapped in the backseat. "There's Mommy's horse," I'd tell the kids. And there he was, now white as snow, grazing and switching at flies. My rides were rare now and even then, my mind would stay focused on the kids, the house and the job.

"It's bad. He's refusing water and he's been down twice." The call came one evening from Lou, who took care of the horses in the field. I was in the middle of making dinner. I called the vet and rushed over. I was shocked at what I saw. Colorado stood unsteadily with head down, his coat rough, his eyes blank. An infection of the lungs had spread and he was seriously dehydrated. It would be impossible to transport him to a barn with electricity where an IV could be started. He was already too far gone.

He was put down the next morning. I squeezed the lead rope when the vet approached with the hypodermic and I sobbed aloud as Colorado jerked his head up with the bite of the needle. He was buried in the same field where he had lived. I watched the rumbling earthmover, so out of place in this quiet field, smooth over his grave. I cried then, not only for the loss of my companion, but also for the loss of my own free-spirited youth and my last link to it. My wild past was buried deeply.

Tracy Van Buskirk

On Call

Hope arouses, as nothing else can arouse, a passion for the possible.

William Sloane Coffin, Jr.

One of my first nights on call started by responding to a page, arriving at the veterinary hospital and rushing into the operating room only to find the lights were out and the room was silent. Suddenly I realized they needed me in the other building where fractures were treated. I had been working as a veterinary technician at a large university hospital for only nine months and my training was still in progress. On this particular night, the only information given was an emergency had arrived that needed my immediate attention. I was calm, yet anxious as I headed in to work.

After realizing where I was needed, I hurried up the hill to discover the usual activity associated with the arrival of a serious fracture. Doctors and nurses rushed in and out of the recovery stall off of the orthopedic surgery room. The patient was having blood drawn and a catheter placed so that intravenous fluids could be given. A surgery resident held a stethoscope to the animal's chest, listening intently.

As I entered the stall, it surprised me to see our patient for the first time. There stood a tiny pony no more than 11-hands tall. She was fuzzy all over looking like something out of a storybook with her fat belly, shaggy mane and tail and long whiskers. The only thing out of place was the unnatural angle at which she held her right hind leg. As I came closer, I realized she was shaking and sweating even though the night was cool.

As I approached, I heard her family talking to her, their voices quiet and serious, "It's okay, Mama, we love you, the doctors are going to fix you right up," chirped a small child. Her name was Daisy and the pony she crooned to was a twenty-eight-year-old with a fractured tibia.

A fractured tibia on a human being is serious, but on a horse, it usually means the death sentence. Mama's age was against her but what Mama had going for her was her size, she probably only weighed about 500 pounds and was so low to the ground that we would be able to assist her as she attempted to stand after surgery without torqueing and possibly re-fracturing the leg. It was this reason and this reason only that gave the doctors hope that they would be able to help Mama. Her family included Mom, Dad, Daisy and her twin brothers, Will and Matt, who were as worried as their younger sister about the seriousness of the pony's condition.

Looking wide-eyed and terrified, Daisy turned to her father and asked, "Daddy, you won't let Mama die, will you?" That look in her eyes tugged on everyone's heart. I knew we would be working all night to save Mama.

Now that the stage was set, we moved into high gear. An orthopedic case like this one is very involved requiring many surgical instruments and supplies. I rushed into Central Supply, the area where all of our surgical instruments are kept, and I quickly set to work putting the supplies on a stainless steel cart, which I then rolled into the surgery room where the anesthesia technician was setting up her equipment. Working with us that night were two surgery residents and because this was such a difficult case, a senior surgeon.

As the clock moved toward 1:00 a.m., preparations finally came to a close. The induction of anesthesia began and I set to work getting Mama ready for the most significant few hours of her life. Positioning the animal on the surgery table is the most critical aspect of the patient prep. Horses that weigh upwards of 1,200 pounds run the risk of permanent nerve damage if they are not positioned perfectly. Once we had Mama positioned appropriately, I commenced clipping her leg. After the clipping came the vacuum cleaner, sucking up Mama's shaggy hair from the surgery area and the floor. "Caps and masks," I sang out as I began to wash Mama's leg with warm water and antiseptic. Everyone scurried off to get their hats and masks.

Obviously, Mama lived outside all year round. Her entire body was covered with caked-on mud and her tail filled with cockleburs. As the warm soapy water ran down her leg onto the surgery table and ultimately the floor, Mama's skin began to get clean. Under that hair and dirt, I discovered a lovely pink leg that began to look as though someone could perform surgery on it. With the final prep completed, I moved quickly to opening the sterile surgery table and instruments. The doctors arrived gloved and gowned and we settled into the surgery.

The night marched on slowly, one hour ticked by and then another. Mama was doing well under anesthesia but the surgeons soon discovered that poor Mama's leg had shattered into five or six pieces. As a resident held the pieces in place, the senior surgeon worked to attach the rest of the pieces like a long thin jigsaw puzzle. Screws were positioned to attach a seven-hole stainless steel plate to Mama's tibia. Once the plate was secured, the surgery site could be closed. It was debatable whether this repair would hold and everyone was thinking the same thought, "This effort can't be in vain, Mama has to make it!"

At 5:30, the bandage was on and we were all bleary-eyed as Mama was moved into the recovery area. As I wheeled the cart of used instruments into sterilizing, the anesthesia tech settled in on the floor of the recovery stall next to Mama, monitoring her vital signs and ready to assist her when it came time for Mama to stand. The ensuing minutes would be crucial to Mama's long-term recovery.

While I cleaned and washed the instruments, members of the surgical team waited anxiously in the stall with Mama. After about half an hour, she began to stir. First, she picked up her head and then she gingerly began to move her legs. After a few more minutes, she rolled and sat up. Now her head was up and she looked at us with eyes that said, "What happened? Where am I and who in the heck are you people?" Her sweat- and urine-soaked coat was plastered to her body from hours of lying on the table. She had the look of someone who had just returned from an all night binge.

Thankfully, she was a clever pony and seemed to know it was best to just stay put for now until the room stopped spinning and she could figure out how to get her feet under her again. Eventually, she deliberately extended her front feet out in front of her and made a mighty heave. With a surgeon pulling on her tail and the anesthetist steadying her head, Mama pulled herself back to vertical, a place she hadn't been for the past six hours. At first, she was wobbly and refused to move, but before long, she began to whinny and take a few careful steps around the recovery stall.

Once Mama seemed a bit surer of herself, we carefully ushered her to her stall in the barn. This was a slow process since she wasn't certain about her ability to walk, but eventually we got her into the stall with a full water bucket, a thick bed of clean straw and a mound of fresh hay in the corner.

Mama's family had waited all night in the lobby to see how she would do and were soon alerted that now was the time they could come and see their pony. One of the barn nurses escorted them to her stall. Young Daisy threw her arms around Mama's neck and buried her face in her mane. "Oh, Mama, you made it!" she sobbed. The rest of the family crowded around, tears streaming down their faces as Mama nickered in response. I couldn't hold back my own tears, the memories of the long, arduous night fading as I watched them scratch Mama's neck and feed her carrots.

The recovery from a major fracture is usually long and slow. The possibility of infection is significant and no one can truly predict the outcome. Somehow, with Mama I had the feeling that things would go well. As it turned out, her hospital stay was brief, only a week, where some horses can take months.

One spring day the following year, one of the residents from the team stopped me as I was setting up for surgery. With a huge smile on his face he said, "Amy, here's something I thought you might like to see."

He handed me a letter from Mama's family with a picture enclosed of Mama with Daisy mounted proudly on her back. The sheer happiness that shone on that little girl's face was so obvious that I almost didn't need to read the letter. Mama had a full recovery and was back to her beloved pastime, trotting around a riding ring teaching youngsters to ride.

Anne Hope

The Little Clydesdale That Could

Today I feel like a sky-high pair of platforms in a closet full of flats.

Jennifer Chambers

Frost's Erastus Sally was a short mare standing only 16 hands, so as a Clydesdale show horse she didn't have a future in the show ring. Nonetheless, Sally distinguished herself from other Clydesdales in a unique way. She became the only show jumping Clydesdale in the Midwest, if not the United States of America.

We started training in October of 1994 and by February we were at our first show. "How exciting this is," the look on Sally's face seemed to say. The thought of a beer horse actually jumping a fence amused the audience, but laughter gave way to stunned silence as Sally completed the Jumper course without dropping a rail and doing the timed jump-off at the fastest speed. May 1995 found us successfully showing Sally in the Jumper ring where she continued winning championships and blue ribbons throughout the show season. Sally enjoyed the crowds and loved to jump, the bigger the better.

Of all the horses I have ever owned, ridden, jumped or done equitation on, Sally was probably the best. She moved like a cat, very smooth and elegant and she was also very protective of her human. When I made a mistake going over a jump and took a bad fall, there she stood, her head by mine, refusing to leave me as I lay on the ground waiting for help to arrive. When they were able to drag her away and head back to the barn, she nickered as she left the ring. Sally continued her show season with another rider in the irons and by the end of the summer, she moved up to the big jumps. After her appearance on ESPN, she was known across America and had fans everywhere. The mare who was too small for her breed standard served as an ambassador for the uniqueness and versatility of the Clydesdale.

Sally instantly became the star when she showed up at a horse show. Once, a woman in a BMW drove up to us waving her hand asking, "Is that Sally, the Jumping Clydesdale?" Never one to disappoint a fan, Sally graciously accepted the woman's offer of a carrot and a scratch on the nose. Throughout her show career, she earned many blues and championships and was mentioned in numerous articles in horse magazines. Sally had made her mark on the show world, but what she meant to our family was so much more than accolades and ribbons.

While carrying my son, Sally had the endearing habit of putting her head down at my belly to feel him move. One day while turning my young gelding out, he kicked me in the head. I went down. Uncertain of how badly I was hurt, I didn't move. Immediately, Sally began speaking horse and stomping to the gelding, keeping him at bay until help arrived. Sally saved my unborn son and me from further, more serious injury from my rambunctious gelding who knew no better.

At the age of fifteen, Sally went lame and we turned her out to pasture to enjoy a well-deserved retirement. The final day she was with us, I put my son on her. She nuzzled his leg and stood quietly as if she knew the intimate connection they shared. Oddly, the day after Sally peacefully went over the rainbow, a newborn fawn and her mom appeared at my back door. As I watched these gentle creatures graze on tender grass, the fawn noticed me and gave me a strangely familiar look. It suddenly struck me where I had seen that expression before and when I acknowledged her as "Sally," she went back to her momma and friends. Whether the moment between us was simply my way of coping with the loss of an irreplaceable member of our family or a truly magical message from my friend, it was no less a comfort to know Sally was still watching over us.

Dawn Stumm

Those Chosen by the Horse

From first sight your gaze is captured, you feel an emotion like you've never known. It's something that grabs a hold of your heart and whispers to you down in your soul.

It hints softly of feelings of wonder and of surprise, of pleasure and of deep peace. And bids you to watch as this wonderful creature dances on air, as though he has wings on his feet.

It speaks quietly to you then, of his beauty and of his grace, whether he is at rest or in full flight. And you feel awed by the mighty but gentle strength he possesses, as he weaves in and out of your sight.

It speaks clearly to you now, telling you to notice his courage and fire and the untamed spirit that is shining in his eyes. Then he commands your attention as he calls out his challenge to the world and you listen wistfully as it echoes up to the skies.

Now . . . if you again feel that tug at your heart and you still hear a whisper of that something unknown, have appreciation that life, as you knew it, has changed somehow and from now on, he has made you his own.

Valerie Shull

A Final Texas Sunset

I will welcome happiness as it enlarges my heart; yet I will endure sadness for it opens my soul. I will acknowledge rewards for they are my due; yet I will welcome obstacles for they are my challenge.

Og Mandino

I looked down the list of appointments, mentally checking off items I would need for each farm visit. Being a horse vet meant long hours traveling down country roads, and I couldn't afford to circle back for forgotten supplies.

The last appointment caught my eye: "Mrs. Deerfield—old horse. 1 mile past Pete's grocery, turn right on county road 327, then take third road to left. Look for sign."

My receptionist was good about giving me landmarks to follow. Most of my clients were backyard horse owners, with three to five acre ranchettes located in outlying communities. It was easy to make a wrong turn and find myself in the middle of nowhere and worse, behind schedule!

I placed the list inside my metal clipboard, grabbed my medical bag and headed for the practice truck. The old Chevy sat with a perpetual rear hunch due to the large fiberglass veterinary box inserted in its bed.

As I drove my rounds, I marveled at the splashes of road-side color from the bluebonnets and other wildflowers heralding the spring season in Texas. My calls were routine, mostly vaccinations, a few deworming and a couple of colt castrations. When I drove past Pete's grocery and turned onto 327, it was 5:00 p.m. and the sun squatted on the horizon. Sunsets in Texas can be beautiful; this one was going to be spectacular.

A wrought iron sign marked the entrance to the Deerfield residence. An avid gardener, I admired the neatly mowed lawn framing the graveled drive, its deep green punctuated with occasional, well-tended flowerbeds. The small frame house at the end of the drive was old but as lovingly cared for as the entrance. A huge pink climbing rosebush framed the screened porch door. Standing on the steps was an elderly, white-haired lady with skin pinched and lined by long hours in the sun.

As she approached my truck, I saw her eyes were a vivid blue, matching the spring sky. She moved slowly, her back bent slightly with age.

"Good afternoon. You must be Dr. Godfrey." A warm smile deepened the wrinkles around her eyes. She was dressed in denim, a pair of battered work boots on her feet.

"Yes, I'm Dr. Godfrey. I've come about your horse. He's not doing well?" I pulled my bag from the seat and closed the truck door.

"No, Buck isn't doing well and I'm worried about him. He's getting on in years, just like me." She smiled again, then turned and began walking toward the barn behind the house.

"How old is Buck, Mrs. Deerfield?" I admired the pro-fusion of flowers in the manicured beds next to the house.

"Oh, he must be at least forty-five by now." She replied matter-of-factly.

"Forty-five!" I tried not to let my voice betray my shock, but a 45-year-old horse was the equivalent of a 135-year-old person!

"Yes, I'm fairly sure of his age. He was a yearling when I bought him for my late husband. Earl used to like to rodeo, so I gave him Buck as a tenth anniversary gift." She stopped to pick a weed from one of the flowerbeds.

"We were married fifty-four years before Earl passed away this fall, so I figure that would make Buck about forty-five. He hasn't been the same since Earl died."

As we approached the barn, I noticed the care that had been lavished on the old building. There was some paint peeling but the structure looked solid and the roof was new. Climbing roses, this time in shades of brilliant red, covered both sides of the door. In a stall toward the rear stood my patient, a bay Quarter Horse gelding. I looked over the stall door and could see Mrs. Deerfield's claim about Buck's age was accurate. The years showed in the white around his muzzle and in the deep sway of his back. He stood with one rear leg cocked and his head drooping toward the floor, fast asleep in the typical resting position of horses.

"Buck, we have a visitor." Mrs. Deerfield's voice was warm with affection as she unlatched the stall door.

"Buck doesn't hear well. He startles if I come up on him too quickly, so I try to make some noise before I walk in his stall." With that, the elderly woman picked up a small metal can and rattled it gently against the door.

Buck's head flew up and he swayed sideways as he pricked his ears toward the sound. Mrs. Deerfield entered the stall, carefully picking her way across the straw.

"He wouldn't hurt a fly, but I have to be careful nowadays. It's just him and me living here and if I fall and hurt myself, no one would know for hours. And if I get hurt, who'd take care of Buck?" She drew a halter around his head and, with measured steps, began walking him toward the door.

"Mrs. Deerfield, let me take him." I was uneasy at the sight of the frail woman handling the unsteady horse. I took the lead rope and petted the old fellow's head while she exited the stall, then carefully guided Buck out the barn door into the sunshine.

The bright light revealed even more signs of ageing, as well as a disturbingly swollen abdomen. The sockets above Buck's eyes were deep and the skin on his face stretched tautly over the bones. His ribs were showing, despite the swollen belly and his hair coat had a dull, lifeless look to it. I shook my thermometer and raising his tail, gently inserted it.

"As I told you, Doctor, Buck hasn't been the same since Earl died, but it's gotten worse over the last month. He's not cleaning up his feed and won't even touch his hay. I'm afraid he might be wormy. Earl used to worm him regularly, but I haven't kept up with it very well."

I withdrew the thermometer and observed the reading, slightly below normal. I placed my stethoscope against Buck's chest. His outward calm was deceptive. Buck's heart rate was almost eighty beats per minute, much faster than I'd expect from a horse at rest. I raised his upper lip and saw the angled, worn teeth typical for his advanced age. His gums were a dark, muddy color instead of pink and when I pushed my thumb against them, it was several seconds before his circulation restored the area with blood.

The diagnosis was not good. Buck's heart was failing and there was a strong probability his kidneys and liver were failing as well. He had beaten the odds, living twice the normal life expectancy for a horse; but his time was running out.

I glanced across at the old woman and took a deep breath. This was one part of my job I truly hated. "Mrs. Deerfield, Buck's condition is much worse than you think. His heart is failing and I'm concerned his other organs are shutting down as well."

Tears welled up in the old lady's eyes and slid down her wrinkled cheeks. Her hand, knobby and twisted from arthritis, lovingly stroked the old horse's neck.

"I suspect he just really misses Earl and wants to be with him. They were inseparable." Closing her eyes, she continued to stroke the old horse. I suspected she was remembering happier times with Earl and Buck. For several moments, we stood silently in the late afternoon sunshine.

Finally, she turned to me, drying her eyes on a lace-edged handkerchief she'd drawn from her pocket.

"Well, I don't want Buck to suffer. Earl would never forgive me if I let that happen." She paused and then spoke so quietly I barely heard, "Do you think it's best to put him down?"

I rubbed Buck's head. "I'm afraid there is nothing else I can do for him. As you said, we don't want him to suffer. It would be kinder to put him down before he gets much worse."

She leaned her head against Buck's neck as more tears moistened her eyes.

"My husband died of cancer, Dr. Godfrey. He lived for about four months after the doctors told us the diagnosis and tried to get his affairs in order as best he could. Before he died, he had an old friend and neighbor of ours dig a place by that tree to bury Buck when the time came." She raised her head and pointed toward a lone oak tree in the far corner of the pasture. "I'd always hoped Buck would die naturally." The next words came as a soft whisper, "Can you do it now?"

I nodded and walked slowly back to my truck, giving Mrs. Deerfield and Buck a few final moments alone. After filling a syringe with the euthanasia solution, I placed it in my pocket and retraced my steps.

When I reached Mrs. Deerfield, she handed me the lead rope. "I hope you don't mind if I go inside while you do it, Dr. Godfrey. I've said my good-byes and I don't think I could . . ." she glanced tearfully toward the pasture, her meaning clear. "Our neighbor should be home before long. He'll come over with his tractor to finish burying him if you'll just put him down near that tree." I nodded, unable to speak as I grappled with my own emotions. She smiled, patted my arm in thanks, then turned and moved slowly toward the house, her back more bent with age than when I'd arrived.

I waited until she'd closed the back door, then gently

aroused the old horse and walked him to the oak tree. Near it was a large piece of plywood covering a deep pit. I stood Buck near the grave and gently inserted the needle into his neck vein. I attached the syringe, carefully injected the solution, then backed to the end of the lead rope as Buck began to sway from the drug's effect. His knees buckled and he sank to the ground. In less than a minute, he was gone. Tears moistened my eyes as I knelt beside his head and gently closed his eyelids. I placed my stethoscope against his chest and listened to the silence. After gathering my things, I returned slowly to my truck. Opening the door, I found a small bouquet of pink roses lying on the seat.

The sunset was as spectacular as I had imagined; long fingers of crimson, purple and gold reaching out across the horizon. The wind had picked up and clouds raced along like yearling colts in a pasture. Looking skyward, I couldn't help but feel somewhere up there an old cowboy named Earl had just been reunited with his best friend.

Jeanna C. Godfrey, D.V.M.

2

HORSES AS TEACHERS

As the traveler who has lost his way, throws his reins on his horse's neck, and trusts to the instinct of the animal to find his road, so must we do with the divine animal who carries us through this world.

Ralph Waldo Emerson

Bending the Rules

*P*ain *nourishes courage. You can't be brave if you've only had wonderful things happen to you.*

Mary Tyler Moore

Not quite six years ago, I flew from New Mexico to Kansas to try a horse with my horse trainer, a woman I'd met just two months prior. My previous riding experience consisted of riding school horses on occasional trail rides and briefly owning an un-broke Arab who tossed me in the dirt more times than I ever want to remember. I was, in very polite horse lingo, green. Not only did I know nothing about trying a horse, I hadn't a clue about eventing, the competitive horse sport I had viscerally chosen to pursue.

The horse's owner met us at the airport and drove us out to his barn. He and my trainer talked old times and business while I changed my clothes, got the horse and walked to an indoor arena. The owner left us to ourselves as soon as I mounted. My trainer turned head-on to the horse and me, silently focused her attention and eagle eyes, and then told me to walk, trot and canter in circles.

"Good," I remember her saying, "The owner's getting his

four-wheeler. We'll drive out to the cross-country area. You just follow us at the walk."

I just nodded, too intimidated by the whole experience to respond out loud. Once there, she told me to go over some jumps. We did.

"Good," she said again, "The two of us are going back to the barn. You go for a hack."

The broad-blazed, burnt-orange, chestnut Quarter Horse and I headed out. The sparkling, filtered light intensified, almost animated, the meadows of full-leafed trees and still running creeks. A chorus comprising assorted birdsongs, the horse's four-beat footfall and my seat's back and forth rubbing against the saddle leathers filled the pungent, fall air. I remember thinking at the time, *I'm doing, right now, this very instant, something I've dreamed of doing my entire life!* I must have gotten lost in time and fantasy because my trainer and the owner came back on the four-wheeler looking for us. "Where have you been?" she asked. "Are you all right?"

"Never better," I beamed.

On the flight back to New Mexico that same day, my trainer said she thought the horse and I were a good match and that she'd like my okay to get the horse vetted. "Fine," I said. I didn't know what getting a horse vetted meant either.

That same week, my husband and I, with our two dogs, drove up to Colorado. Friday, I had a bilateral mastectomy. Eight days later, my trainer called. I was still semiconscious from being unable to take pain medication but I wanted to hear about the horse. She must have talked details about vet results but all I remember her saying was that she thought we ought to get him. All I recall my saying was that I wanted the horse to be at her barn in two weeks.

"Why two weeks?" she wanted to know.

"Because I'll be back in two weeks. I need him to be there when I am."

Two weeks later, the horse and I met again in New Mexico. Three weeks after that—and no, I did not tell my doctor—I got on my new horse, Red. It was obvious, even to green me, that Red knew more about most things than most riders and most horses will ever know about anything. But mostly, Red knew that I couldn't fall off him. Any fall, for any reason would have ripped apart the not-yet-healed stitches that were holding my chest together.

Three weeks after that, I realized that everyone riding at my barn was going to a show in Arizona. I told my trainer I wanted to go. Our conversation went something like . . . "Great, it would be great for you to come with us and watch."

"No," I said, "I don't want to watch. I want to ride."

"What?" She laughed out loud. "Are you crazy?"

I didn't say anything.

"You're serious, aren't you?" She seemed stunned. "You don't know anything about riding! You don't know the first thing about eventing!" she continued. "You just had this surgery! You are crazy!"

I didn't say anything again.

Finally, looking down at the ground, my trainer whispered, "Is everything okay with you?"

"No. It isn't."

Neither of us said a word for a very long time.

Slowly, very slowly, she said, "I'll think about it. What you're asking me here goes against everything I know. Everything I've learned in thirty-five years."

"How long are you going to think?" I asked.

"I'll tell you my decision tomorrow."

Three weeks later, my husband and I, Red and our two dogs caravanned with everyone else from the barn to the horse trial in Arizona. Even after daily lessons to get me ready, I still wasn't sure about the geometry of a twenty meter circle. I was even less sure that I'd be able to remember the dressage test I was supposed to ride. It turned out that I didn't. To top off the day I got lost in stadium jumping, didn't hear or even know anything about a disqualifying whistle and didn't leave that arena until Red and I had jumped every jump of our course. I heard two years later that my trainer had buried her head in her hands during our round.

The next day, Red and I entered the start box for cross-country. My trainer, unknown to me, had begged the event organizer to let me ride the course despite rendering myself ineligible in stadium jumping. I remember thinking at the time that cantering over logs and rocks and into water on a horse was the most exciting thing I had ever set out to do. It turned out that it was. When we got to fence fifteen, an open arrowhead the likes of which I hadn't seen during my three weeks of training leading up to the competition, I said to Red, out loud, "I don't know what to do here. But you do. Just remember, I can't fall off."

I'd swear to this day that Red said, "Fine."

I gave him the reins and we went. Three more fences after that and we completed the course. Clean and clear.

My family was just beyond the finish line, yelling and barking. I slid off Red, burst into tears and wrapped myself in my husband's arms and the dogs' slathering tongues.

"I'm alive," I sobbed.

Now, not quite six years later, I'm still learning dressage geometry, still occasionally getting lost in a stadium round and still absolutely ecstatic jumping cross-country courses. My trainer and I are still together, now as good friends as well as crazy student and eagle-eyed trainer.

Red died a few months ago. A benign cyst turned malignant. When we were both cancer free, he "pre" and me "post," that broad-blazed, burnt-orange, chestnut Quarter Horse found me in the air time after time after time. And time after time after time, Red taught me to find the verb "to live" inside the phrase "being alive."

Janet Steinberg

God's Gift

If one advances confidently in the direction of his dreams and endeavors to live the life which he has imagined, he will meet with a success unexpected in common hours.

Henry David Thoreau

I believe that God gives us hints of what we will find in heaven through the gifts he gives us here on earth. My greatest glimpse of heaven came at a time when I felt the farthest away from God's grace, in the form of a 16-hand sorrel Quarter Horse named Chex.

My family moved to northern Idaho when I was in the seventh grade. It was a terrible time for me, filled with heartbreak and loneliness. I had few friends, I was plagued with shyness and I was far larger than the popular girls in school. Everything in life seemed to be against me. My parents encouraged me to pursue horseback competition to make up for my lack of athletic ability in any school sport. So I entered Chex, my thirteen-year-old horse, into the 4-H horse division. The idea that Chex, an aged, used Quarter Horse could even come close to winning a grand championship in Western pleasure was a complete joke. He was a retired roping and pack horse with the personality of a Labrador retriever and had more miles on him than our farm's beat-up old pickup truck.

My first day of 4-H was worse than I could ever have imagined. Not only was I totally left out of the close-knit circles of friends already formed, but I had no idea how to ride Western pleasure. It was clear that these teams were well-trained and rehearsed. My wild and completely uncontrolled lap around the arena was more of a rodeo ride than anything resembling a show-horse performance. Hunched wide-eyed over Chex's neck and clutching the saddle horn for dear life, I bounced a foot out of the saddle with every jolt of Chex's fast-gaited, roping-horse jog.

I heard the muffled giggles and felt the hard stares from other riders in the arena as I tugged on Chex's reins. He immediately came to an abrupt halt, almost throwing me over his head, which only added to my embarrassment. Defeated, I led Chex back to our trailer, avoiding everyone's gaze including my mom's. "Now honey, this is only your first time in the show arena," Mom consoled me, "Most of these girls could ride before they could walk." Her words barely registered and I ignored the playful nudge from Chex's muzzle.

That night lying in bed, I looked out my window and stared into the endless starlit north Idaho sky. I thought of that distant God I knew only superficially from my childhood Bible study classes. "God," I said, my voice shaking with emotion, "I know we don't talk much, but I need your help." I prayed that God would help me find happiness and friendship. I asked Him to let me find myself and where I belonged. I felt so lost.

The next day at school was no different from the horrible ones that had preceded it. I rode home on the bus feeling alone and totally ignored by everyone, including God. I stepped off the bus, my head hanging as low as my spirits and I heard Chex's familiar nicker. I looked up to see him prancing alongside the pasture fence as if beckoning me to ride him. Chex's head was held Arabian high, his red mane flowed behind him in undulant waves and his feet were lifting in a joyful dance, hardly touching the ground.

My eyes widened and in that moment, I felt different. It was like seeing Chex for the first time and in a completely new way. He wasn't a used-up roping horse that couldn't compete with the other horses. I saw a loving and spirited companion who wanted to share the fun and beauty in life with me; he was an angel, sent by God to heal my heart. I dropped my backpack and began brushing Chex's thick, furry coat with my bare hands. I grabbed his halter, swung myself onto him and rode him bareback in our sand arena.

As we loped around the arena, my worries and hurt vanished. The only reality that remained was that of girl and horse. Breathing deeply, I inhaled the pure scent of pine trees and horsehair. As we pulled to a stop in the middle of the arena, I leaned forward and threw my arms around Chex's neck in a loving hug. I felt joy, something that had been buried deep inside me under the invisible wounds and painful problems that I'd carried alone since childhood.

That day marked a new chapter in my life. I began to see the beauty and grace in the world around me. Each day, I'd race home from school to ride my four-footed friend who always greeted me with the same joyful nicker. Chex became my confidante; his wise, deep-brown eyes comforted and soothed me in ways that words never could. I was still an awkward and uncoordinated teenager with frizzy hair and extra chub, but something inside of me was different. At the weekly 4-H meetings, I no longer worried about what other people thought of me. I kept my attention fixed on riding Chex and I gained a new confidence in life. I had found unconditional acceptance in Chex, who loved me whether or not I was deemed "cool," or was an all-star athlete or boy magnet.

The night before our county fair, the pinnacle of local 4-H competition, I hopped up on Chex's bare back. The sun set over the mountains as we loped around the arena and I felt the same joy and freedom as I had the day after my prayer. I closed my eyes, feeling Chex's muscles rippling beneath me and the cool breeze rushing past us, serenaded by the intensifying humming of the crickets. "Lord, help us tomorrow, give us faith in ourselves," I prayed.

We arrived at the fair. My heart pounded and my stomach lurched as Chex and I entered the arena at a jog behind the other polished riders. I gripped the reins with shaking hands and my legs wobbled helplessly in the stirrups. Luckily, Chex was on autopilot. Making up for my seeming paraplegia, he took over dancing around the arena, ears pricked forward, his deep brown eyes sparkling. The entire year's work had come down to this moment. It was our chance to prove ourselves. I glanced down at Chex and I felt his spirit fill me. Suddenly it was just us again, a girl and a horse loping bareback and free in an arena. A smile spread across my face as a new peace enveloped me, diminishing my fears.

When the class ended and all the horses lined up in the middle of the arena, I couldn't wipe the grin off my face. As the judge walked down the line placing her marks, I realized that I had erased all thoughts of competition from my mind. Although touching your horse while the judge was finalizing the scores was taboo, I snuck a pat to Chex's neck and whispered a thank you. Instantly, his right ear pivoted backwards to acknowledge and receive it.

The judge approached me, a smile on her face. "Well Missy, I can't say you or your horse were the most practiced Western pleasure pair I've ever seen, but you definitely have something that the other riders didn't. You have a love and happiness that reminds me of myself when I was young. Never lose that," she said, giving Chex's neck a pat.

We exited the arena with only a red ribbon, but I couldn't have been more proud. What did a blue ribbon matter? I had already been given the top prize, a best friend named Chex.

Mikkel Becker

The Will to Survive

The air of heaven is that which blows between a horse's ears.

Arabic saying

It was May of 1996 when we moved to our new home on the outskirts of Reno, Nevada. Our house was situated on a rise that overlooked Reno to the west and an area called Hidden Valley to the east. I had heard of the wild horses that roamed Hidden Valley and hoped for the opportunity to see them. Alas, all I saw for months were street signs that warned motorists, "Wild Horse Crossing."

One night towards the end of August, our dog started barking wildly at the front door. When I first stepped onto the front porch, I saw nothing but darkness and the dim twinkle of lights in the distance. As I continued down the stairs and onto the driveway, I heard the faintest of unidentifiable sounds. Although I saw nothing, something told me I was not alone.

My eyes finally adjusted to the dark and the silhouettes of horses began to take form. Thirteen wild horses were munching grass on my front lawn. At first, I was afraid to move. Who wants to spook a bunch of wild horses when you are standing in the middle of them? I stood there for what seemed like an eternity. I was totally and completely mesmerized. I went to bed that night, leaving the horses to eat their fill and feeling more peaceful than I had in years. The next morning found me wide-eyed and anxious to see my new friends. They were nowhere to be found. One sighting was all I got. What a disappointment!

Fall of '97 rolled around and still no horses. It seemed everyone else had seen them but me. Christmas was approaching and my gift was to come early that year. My mother and husband presented me with a new camera. The first weekend I had free we were off on a search for the wild horses. A neighbor told me of a dirt road that would take us into the hills east of our home. It turned out to be a day I'll never forget.

We came upon three bands of horses spaced out along a dirt path. I walked past the first band in order to place the sun at my back. As a result, the other two bands were also at my back. I was so engrossed by what I saw through the viewfinder that I was oblivious to what was going on behind me. Out of nowhere I felt a puff of hot air on my shoulder then a nudge on my side. I turned to find myself surrounded by thirty wild horses. Three yearlings and a pregnant mare were sniffing my neck and nibbling at my jacket. Some ignored me completely and others watched with great curiosity.

There I stood surrounded by these wild creatures and being treated as one of the family. Unlike my first experience, there was no anxiety. It was clear they had accepted me as a friend. The yearlings finally got bored and went off to frolic in the sagebrush. The pregnant mare took one more nibble at my jacket then abruptly turned and led the bands away. I stood for some time watching them literally walk into the sunset. My heart was so full I thought it would burst. That was the first day of a new passion for me. Every weekend, every holiday and any other day I could get free was spent searching for the wild horses.

Winter was busy for the wild-horse advocates who ran an emergency feed program from October though April. Close to one hundred wild ones used the area as their wintering grounds. In February we were on our way to find our favorite harem band when I noticed a very young filly standing alone between a bachelor band and another harem band. It wasn't until after we passed that I realized there was something wrong with that picture. We continued on our way but I couldn't get it out of my mind. I knew the harem band and they had no new fillies. She certainly did not belong to the bachelors. Who was she? Where did she come from? When we came back that way, the two bands were still there but the filly was gone.

To this day, I don't know what possessed me. I insisted that we stop. I walked a good 300 yards into the desert and there she was lying in the dirt. Her eyes grew wide and full of fear when she saw me. She tried to flee but couldn't get up. We observed her from a distance for a while. Daylight would be gone soon and the other horses were beginning to graze their way toward the watering hole. We could hear the howl of coyotes close by. This was no place for an injured filly to be alone. It was time for a rescue.

The rescue crew arrived in less than an hour. It was dusk now and oh, so cold. The vet advised us that her chances of survival were not good. She was extremely emaciated and it appeared as though her hind legs were at least partially paralyzed. An attempt to save her life would be costly and there could be no guarantees.

Wild horse advocates come from all walks of life. We're quite the diverse bunch of coconuts. The one thing that binds us is a deep love and respect for these magnificent animals. I was the first to break the silence with a donation toward the cause. The others quickly followed.

My husband and I were left to guard the filly while the others tackled the not-so-easy task of arranging for a horse trailer to make its way over such unforgiving terrain. The harem band had already disappeared and the bachelors were well on their way. We watched as one young bachelor broke from his friends and made his way back to our filly. He whinnied, then grabbed her by the scruff of her neck in an attempt to get her up. We could imagine him saying, "Come on, friend, we're leaving now. It's time to go." She tried again and again but couldn't get up. The young bachelor was determined. He wasn't going to leave her. With each failed attempt to get her on her feet, he got more insistent and a little rougher. Worried that he was doing more harm than good, we finally shooed him away.

It was several hours before our filly was on her way to medical care. I dreamed of her and the young bachelor that night. I'll always wonder about the bond that tied them. I knew our wild ones well and she did not belong. Tick paralysis had caused her to go down that day. Aside from being emaciated, she was infested with ticks and worms. The name Bugz fit her well. She was also much too young to be away from mother's milk. What had happened? Where did she come from?

Her story began to unfold in the next few days. And what a story it was! Two days after last Christmas, members of our rescue crew had been the first to be called by Washoe County Animal Control when thirty-four wild horses were discovered slaughtered in a valley just east of our home. Three young men were eventually tried and given suspended sentences and minimal fines—a slap on the wrist for using live animals as target practice. When all the facts were in, it was determined that our little filly had been a part of that massacre!

We will never know what went on during those two months. She was only four months old when her family was destroyed. She wandered from one valley to the next, alone and slowly starving. What a will to survive! Did the young bachelor somehow know of her trials? Did Pegasus hold her up just long enough for a wild horse lover like me to spot her?

Bugz was not returned to the wild, as she would not have survived, but today she is free from haunting memories and now enjoying life romping with a rescued wild colt called Spirit in Carson City, Nevada. A beautiful creature; truly a survivor.

Carrol Abel

When the Student Becomes the Teacher

The risk to remain tight in the bud is more painful than the risk it takes to blossom.

Anais Nin

"If you'll sit back more, it will help your horse get off her forehand." I grit my teeth and attempt to lift my upper body up and back the requisite amount, all the while keeping the trotting horse moving forward.

"Your arms are locked. You've got to relax your shoulders and allow your horse to move. That's why she's so tense."

My shoulders are not locked, I want to shout. *The horse is tense because . . . because . . . because she wants to be tense!*

"Do you want me to ride her?"

I pull the mare to a halt, turn and walk over to the rail. A thousand angry words rampage dangerously close to the surface but I swallow them back, wipe the scowl from my face and slide off. "Okay," I say, keeping my voice steady. With forbearance that would have pleased Mother Teresa, I humbly hand the reins over to my daughter.

With glazed eyes I watch as she lithely mounts the 16-hand Thoroughbred, something I haven't been able to do without assistance in years. In moments, the mare has stopped her head tossing and is calmly moving forward. As they move into a springy trot, my daughter sings out, "This trot would get good scores at First Level!"

Wow, how time changes things. Was it only ten years ago that this same child cried every time I tried to get her to canter her pony? Wasn't I the one who taught her how to saddle and bridle that pony, who taught her correct riding position, who encouraged her to see things from the pony's perspective? And yet, here I stand, watching her whirl around the arena on my new horse, my emotions a strange combination of injured pride over my own deficient skills and incredible pride in what I see before me.

For my child has grown. Not just physically, but in subtle, hard-to-define ways. The fearful little girl has given way to a confident young woman who is excelling, not only in her horsemanship, but in other aspects of her life as well. She's learned to work hard, that success doesn't come easily and that fears can be overcome. And much of this growth has occurred, I am convinced, because of her early and continued involvement with horses. But there has been another, quite unexpected, benefit to our shared passion for these large and wonderful creatures.

Heather and I don't see eye-to-eye on many things. I am a talker; she's quiet. I am nostalgic; she's overwhelmingly practical. I am overly concerned with what others think and feel; she really isn't. Often we clash. But our mutual love of horses has opened a door of communication between us that might not have occurred any other way.

We've been to the mountaintop, she and I, literally and figuratively. Thanks to our horses, we've seen sights that many never see and have memories we share with no one else. Most of the memories are good, but some are painful. When that first sassy pony was sold, I don't know who cried more. When my blind Appaloosa died in an accident, Heather didn't say much but I knew she understood.

Life goes on and people change. Healthy relationships grow; they cannot be static and hope to survive. In my less defensive moments, I am thankful for this. Even this reversed relationship of teacher-student has its upsides. In my first dressage show, on her horse, it was Heather who warmed the horse up, handed out coaching tips, read my test and collected that coveted ribbon. Some people pay big bucks for such professional assistance!

But I'm still conflicted. Long before I was a mother, I was a horse lover. I grew up reading *The Black Stallion* and watching *My Friend Flicka* on television every Saturday morning. But I also grew up in a working-class family where the idea of owning something as extravagant as a horse could not even be considered. I remember my father telling my mother to not worry, I would soon grow out of this silly stage. Thirty-plus years later, I still haven't grown out of it!

I did grow up though and followed the path of many well-meaning parents. I tried to give my child all the things I so desperately wanted when I was young. And it's been a good investment; she's doing well, loves her horse and riding and even contemplates horses as a vocation someday. But meanwhile, I'm still standing on the sidelines, wishing I were young and thin and flexible—that I was capable of doing what she now does so effortlessly.

And depression almost overtakes me, until a new thought works its way through the haze of my self-pity. As I remember all the lessons I paid for, all the times I sat watching and listening from the sidelines, it occurs to me that I don't have to feel sorry for myself, that I might still be able to benefit from the years and dollars spent in helping her reach her riding goals. If I can swallow my pride (a big *if*) and listen to what she has to say, I can be a step closer to my own goals, as well. It's a comforting thought.

And not too far down the road, just around the corner, in fact, college and "real life" looms for my daughter. I'll cry when she goes. Then I'll dry my eyes, pull on my boots and head for the barn. Because finally, after all these years, it's going to be my turn!

Dawn Hill

Summer Treasures

No bird soars too high, if he soars on his own wings.

William Black

My last customer's tab had been rung up on the old cash register. I carefully placed the final dirty dish in the holding tray then shoved the tray into the gaping mouth of the huge gleaming steel dishwasher. It was finally quiet, the morning rush over. I had been working since 6 a.m. and my ten-year-old stomach had been rumbling for an hour. "Break time, Janie girl," Anna smiled over her shoulder as she finished cleaning the hot stove with oil and the big rectangular chore stone. "How 'bout I cook you some breakfast?"

I loved Anna's kind face, her sparkling blue eyes and her strong arms that would wrap around me when my mom wasn't looking. Anna had been the morning cook since my parents bought the small town café. Auntie Anna, as I called her, was tall, big boned, thin as a rail and had huge hard-working hands. It was the custom for children raised in the 1950s to call all adults Aunt, Uncle or Mr. or Mrs., never by their first names. Anna had insisted that she was to be my Auntie.

Just as I was about to say "I'd love some pancakes," my mother came into the kitchen with a pie in her hand and a look on her face as cold as the steel sinks. She glared at me, then Anna, put the pie in the oven and stalked out of the kitchen. She had been giving me the silent treatment for two days, ever since my father had told me that I could accept Anna's invitation to work on her ranch in the afternoons for the summer after our work in the café was done. Of course my mother's icy silences, cold withdrawals and statements that I would never amount to anything seemed to need no reason. No matter how hard I worked or tried to seek her approval, I had grown accustomed to the cold climate of inevitable failure, just as I had grown accustomed to my father's unwelcome touches and my parents' late-night whiskey battles.

"Don't pay her any mind, Janie girl," Anna said kindly, "She just isn't in the best of moods this morning. You're a good hardworking girl. Now eat some pancakes, you're going to need some energy for that work waiting for you at the ranch this afternoon." She winked at me.

I will never forget my first glimpse of the Flying W Ranch as we rounded the corner of the dusty dirt road in Anna's old pickup. The ancient, big white farmhouse with a wraparound porch that seemed to radiate as much love as Anna's solid arms. The huge red barn, the corral full of beautiful horses, cattle grazing on what appeared to be endless acreage and Zip, the Australian shepherd that yipped at the tires of the truck.

After we got out of the truck, Anna introduced me to her two boys whom I'd never met, Sandy and Donny, and to her husband, Pete. Then they took me to the corral and introduced me to Fleet Foot, a beautiful black stallion. As I rubbed his silky muzzle and looked into his soft warm brown eyes, I was told that he was one of the finest cutting horses on the ranch and would be mine for the summer.

I worked on the ranch every summer until I left home at eighteen, even though my mother made it so hard for Anna that she finally quit her cooking job when I was twelve. My memories are full of summer afternoons flying through tall grass holding on to the reins while Fleet Foot did his job cutting the cattle. I raced Sandy and Donny bareback across rivers and streams and kneaded bread dough for Auntie Anna while I watched her churn butter. Sitting at the big harvest kitchen table, we said grace before dinner to the sound of Zip lapping the rich cream that Uncle Pete always gave him fresh from the bucket because, "He was a hardworking animal who deserved his share of the best."

I never told Auntie Anna or Uncle Pete the horrors that were going on in my childhood home; I didn't need to, although I often confided my deepest secrets to Fleet Foot and Zip. Many of us carry wounds from our childhood, but many, like me, also carry the treasures and gifts of people along the way who took the time to care.

When my children were young, they helped me make bread once a week and we shared meals around a harvest table like the one in that old farmhouse. Our house was frequently full of extra children and we always had a dog. I hugged my children every day of their lives, and I still love to sit with my grandchildren on the wraparound porch of my home, reveling in warm memories and creating new ones.

Those days on the Flying W were few, but the work I did there was more than cutting cattle and mending fences; the lasting work was the mending of my spirit and the knowledge that, like Zip, we all deserve to be treated with kindness and compassion when we give our best.

Jane Middelton-Moz

Horse D'oeuvres

Every day, my horse needs to be courted
Before he'll deign to let himself be caught.
His enticements need not be imported;
Some carrots from the garden? He'll be bought.

Better yet, apples from the neighbor's yard
Or cubes of sugar from the coffee tray.
Could be worse; he might require caviar.
Then *I'd* have to content myself with hay!

Lawrence Schimel

The Horse That Taught Me to Fly

Skill and confidence are an unconquered army.

George Herbert

The man who shoes our horses, forty-two-year-old Marty Rice, is about 6'3" and weighs 225 pounds. With a tapered torso and sleeve-ripping biceps, Marty looks like Michelangelo's David, only with a cowboy hat and chaps. Rough and tough would be two bull's-eye descriptions for Rice, a local legend when it comes to riding, roping and breaking horses that send most people over the fence in fear.

Marty was at our Almost Heaven Ranch when one of our Quarter Horses, GloLopin, reared backwards and pulled the lead rope off the hitching post so hard and fast that it literally smoked. After we had gathered ourselves and got GloLopin calmed and restrained, I noticed Marty wincing in pain at some of the chiropractic maneuvers required to shoe a horse. I asked Marty what was the matter.

With a smile on his face, Marty told me that a friend of his, Dave Colson, had recently asked him to go to famed Ray Hunt's colt-starting seminar in Wyoming. Marty was unable to go, but asked Dave to bring back the videotape no matter what the cost.

Marty has two boys, Andy and Matt, that are big, buff and love horses just like their dad. As requested, Colson brought the Rices the colt-breaking videotape and Marty and the boys sat down early one evening to watch the tape.

Marty was a big fan of Hunt's and everything on the videotape about breaking colts made perfect sense. It seemed like a miracle when thirty people in a row broke their colts without hardly breaking a sweat, let alone any bones, and rode them off in victory.

The longer the tape went on, the more eager Marty was to stop the tape and start breaking a horse in order to show Andy and Matt just how well this new technique would work on the horses they broke for a living. Yet, Marty was not wanting to break just any old horse, but already had the perfect one in mind.

Outside was a four-year-old stud reigning-bred horse, of championship stock, that Marty described as "having a lot of action." Because nobody had been able to get near Little Double Pine, as he was formally known, let alone on him, Marty was able to purchase him for much less than the asking price. Break him and there was money to be made on this horse.

With dollar bills dancing in his head and newfound confidence swelling his chest, Marty stopped the training tape, jumped up and started putting on his cowboy gear. Yup, Marty was going to go out and demonstrate for the Rice family just how easy and profitable this new colt-breaking technique really was.

Well, Marty's oldest boy, Andy, wasn't quite as confident in the one hour lesson they'd just received on the boob-tube and cautioned his dad, loudly, "Dad, I don't think that horse is ready for this yet and neither are we."

Marty replied with a tip of the hat, "You just watch."

Hearing the commotion, Marty's wife, LaRae, said, with her hands on her hips, "Marty, if you're going to do something stupid let me get the video camera." Marty said, "There ain't time. I'll have the horse broke before you get it ready."

Marty strode through the round pen gate and sallied up to Little Double Pine with the saddle, tossed it on, hooked it up and jumped on to duplicate the effortless horse breaking he'd seen on the tape.

What happened next could best be described as "fast forward."

Little Double Pine started bucking while Marty gave him his head like he'd seen on the Hunt video. About the third buck, Marty lost his hat and started yelling out instructions to the boys.

"Andy, pick up my hat and when I come around hand it to me."

"Matt, run over to the barn and shut off the fencer," which was charging the hot wire they'd run around the inside of the round pen to keep the stud inside.

As Marty made his second circuit of the pen on the bucking horse, he noticed Matt over at the fencer switch and assumed he'd shut it off and the fence was now dead. Marty turned Little Double Pine into the fence knowing he could no longer buck against the panels.

Sensing horse-breaking victory, what Marty didn't realize at that instant was his brother Bill had moved the switch for the fencer when he re-wired the barn and Matt had flipped a switch that no longer worked. The wire running inside the pen was still full of juice and Marty's mount was about to be.

As Marty careened into the fence, his hand hit the hot wire. A gazillion volts coursed into his hand, through his body and out his leg onto the sweaty flanks of the horse.

Instantly, Little Double Pine acquired a gift that wasn't on the video Marty had just watched, a gift he was about to impart to Marty as well. The gift of flight!

The horse vaulted into the air like an Olympic high-jumper and Marty rode him up like an elevator. With his back scraping the clouds, Marty came off Little Double Pine at an odd angle and started heading straight for the murky stock tank, looking like those awkward birds that careen out of the sky and plunge into the ocean targeting an unsuspecting fish.

As Marty's flight path neared the tank he put his hands out to catch the edge of the tank but his momentum jammed his thumbs, knocked his arms back to his sides like folded wings and Marty high-dived, face first, into the stock tank, his right upper torso careening off the hard plastic lip.

Besides his rib cage, what broke Marty's fall was his open mouth sliding along the bottom of the tank until his head hit the side and he stopped. All joking aside, this Rice definitely snapped, crackled and popped.

With the breath knocked out of him and with his arms still behind him, Marty panicked as he thought his own family would see him drown in a 150-gallon Rubbermaid stock tank in his own corral. Finally, Marty righted himself, surfaced, crawled out of the water, bent over, grabbed his knees and tried to squelch the pain in his ribs and thumbs and catch his breath.

Concerned at the unplanned human moon shot and re-entry they'd just witnessed courtesy of dear old dad, the boys yelled out from opposite sides of the round pen, "Are you okay, Dad?!" Marty just gave them a head nod and that's all it took for the boys to break out laughing so hard they nearly cried.

Dried off and loaded up with painkillers (Tylenol and Busch Light), Marty got to tell what it was like to experience what astronauts feel upon launch, how weightless he felt at the zenith of his trajectory and how helpless he felt as he plummeted toward Earth, or water, with no chute. At the end Marty told his boys, "Andy, Matt, have you ever wondered what the bottom of a stock tank tastes like? Well, now I know."

The colt-training video? Gathering dust on its way to a garage sale. The horse? Marty is undecided, but Little Double Pine will have earned a new name. Cessna, for the beginning of the flight or Stock Tank for the ending.

Marty Rice as told to Marty Becker

"I don't think this combination saddle bronk-highdiving
event is such a good idea!"

A Prince of a Horse

Do not wait for great strength before setting out,
for immobility will weaken you further.

Phillipe Vernier

"She's small enough, she could ride Prince," one wrangler said. The other one cast a dubious eye over me and then reluctantly agreed. "She rides better than the rest of them. I guess she could handle him."

"Who's Prince," I asked? I had looked forward to the horsemanship program at Girl Scout camp all summer. Standing hopefully beside a big beautiful chestnut that I had secretly picked out as my mount, my heart fell when the wranglers brought me to another corral and I saw the bay equine that awaited me. A pony, Prince was a pony!

I would never live down the short jokes now. The other girls got tall, beautiful horses and here I was, the short girl who was always teased for being little, stuck with a short, darned pony. It was a moment before I noticed the wrangler was addressing me. "I wouldn't put any of these other girls on Prince," he was telling me, which bolstered my spirits slightly. "But I know you have some riding experience. He's not like these dude horses; he has a mind of his own. Be real careful with him around water."

He hurried off to help the other girls saddle their big, tall, gorgeous horses while I led Prince out and tied him to the hitching post. He rolled an evil eye at me, clearly displeased to be asked to do something. I glared right back at him and saddled him up, struggling to get the horse-size cinch snug around his abdomen. Ready to face my camp mates, I braced myself for the short jokes.

"OOOOH," they squealed. "He's sooooo cute."

"You get to ride a pony? No fair!"

"I want to ride him."

"He's just your size, you look so adorable together."

Prince pulled his first pony moment where a recent rain had left a big puddle of water. I was relieved that he didn't balk before entering the water, so was taken unawares when he then stopped short. When he put his nose down, I thought he wanted to drink and gave him his head. Belatedly, I remembered the wrangler's words as Prince's knees started to buckle and I pulled his head up. He was trying to lie down and roll, with me, the saddle and everything! Thwarted in his desires, he wouldn't leave the mud hole. It took much pounding with heels and slapping of reins to get him moving again.

The trail grew narrow and rocky, wending its way between lodge pole pine and aspen trees, going up and down hills. Coming down the first steep hill, it seemed that the saddle suddenly got a lot closer to Prince's ears. It was then that I realized that the saddle was rolling loosely on his back. I knew I had tightened the cinch! But Prince was apparently good at puffing up his belly and with his round barrel it didn't take much for the saddle to slip. I barely made it to a flat stretch to jump off him and re-tighten the saddle.

With his short little legs, Prince didn't walk as fast as the horses so we got farther and farther behind. While everyone else was walking calmly, I was locked into a battle of strategy with Prince; walking wherever there was a downhill section, then allowing him to trot on the flat and uphill sections to catch up. Whenever I started him into a catch-up trot, there were yells of complaint from the girls on the horses behind me, whose horses also started trotting.

Then we came to the river. It was when the water was up to his chest that Prince stopped in the middle of the stream and started bobbing his head. But I was wise to him and wouldn't give him his head. He started pawing the water in frustration. I couldn't budge him. Kicking did no good because my feet couldn't reach his sides through the water. I needed both my hands to keep his head up and I was nearly dislodged from his back by his vigorous flailing. I could see the wranglers trying to help, only to have their horses shy away from the eruption of water Prince was creating. Finally one got close enough to grab his reins and, spurring her horse, dragged Prince from the water, me clinging to his back. I was sopping from head to foot; the counselors who'd tried to help me were drenched. Only Prince was happy. He stretched out his nose and shook, scattering water everywhere and nearly throwing me from the saddle. Then he grunted and sighed, telling us just how pleased he was with himself.

Soon after the river, we came to the most dangerous part of the trail. Because he couldn't drown me, I guess Prince decided to murder me instead. We were carefully walking along a narrow trail chiseled from the side of the mountain. Prince chose that moment to turn like a gymnast on a balance beam and charge back down the direction we came. I barely got him stopped before he knocked the other horses off the narrow trail like a bowling ball. One misstep and we would all be toast, falling over the side. I could hear the wrangler yelling to me, but with horses between us she couldn't come to our aid. I had to get Prince to back up and turn in the correct direction on that narrow trail. And there was no one there to do it but me. Maybe all the times before when he had tested me had earned me some begrudging respect, because this time he listened to my hands and my voice. He turned on a dime and continued up the trail like nothing had happened.

When we arrived in camp, I was braced for complaints

about my unruly mount disturbing everyone's ride. But instead, all the girls flocked around and admired my "darling" pony. "Ohhhh, he's so cute," they squealed! "He's just adorable," they cooed. "I wish I could ride him," they said wistfully. *Were you on the same ride I was on?* I wanted to ask. *Didn't you see him try to roll me in mud, bolt down the road, fight me all the way when I kept him to a walk, have to trot to keep up, turn into a fountain in the middle of the river, try to drop both me and him in the lake? And you think he's cute?*

After grazing the horses, we were instructed to find a strong tree and tie our horses using a quick release knot. *Finally,* I thought, *something I can do right.* Just as night started to settle over our mountain camp, we hear the cries of "loose horse" and the wranglers all jump up and rush into the dark to catch the wayward beast before it gets hurt. It was Prince, of course. And while some didn't believe that I had tied him tight, I knew at least one did. Apparently, he could untie knots. Now he was double-tied.

The next day Prince was a perfect gentleman on the trail ride home. When we came to the river, we were prepared for him. A wrangler rode on each side of his rump and the moment he hesitated to try to take a bath, they both slapped him with their ropes and he gave up on the idea.

"You know," the counselor told me on the bus ride back to camp, "It wasn't just because you are little that I put you on Prince. He could have easily carried any of these girls, but you had the riding skill to handle him. And, you got a better ride than anyone here because you had to match wits with a very clever pony."

It was a while before I realized what I had learned from Prince on that ride. Society is geared to looking up to the tall guy and down on the short one, often overlooking and under-valuing little people. But those who are small can still be tough and smart—and keep you on your toes. Genghis Kahn almost took over the world on horses no bigger than Prince. It's not how small you are, but how you use it.

Janice Willard, D.V.M., M.S.

Tough Decisions

It's difficult to say goodbye but the memory of being together will always remain and there is always the chance that our paths will cross again.

Donna Yee

The phone is cold and smooth in my hand, as the line disconnects. The appointment is scheduled. Our veterinarian will come in a few days to end the suffering of a dear old friend.

"These old ponies," our vet, Dr. Lisa, says sympathetically, "They hang on and on. So often we hope that they'll just drift away in their sleep, but it hardly ever goes that way. They leave the tough decisions to their people."

This tough decision has been hovering for months now. With several animals over the years, I've never found it easy to know: Is this life still enjoyable, worth living? Or have we let an animal suffer silently and trustingly, too long in pain? Late last winter, we saw that Cricket, our ancient pony, was declining. In our wet Northwest climate, the chill of winter just seeps into those elderly bones, stiffening joints beyond use. Our thirteen-year-old daughter, Caroline, found Cricket out in the field one day, lying down on her side in a cold drizzling rain. With much coaxing and encouragement, she convinced Cricket to heave herself up on swollen arthritic legs and led her slowly to the shed to dry, draped with a warm blanket.

Caroline returned to the house in tears. We had mentioned the possibility before, but now we talked in earnest about calling Dr. Lisa to come with the final injection to end the pain and struggle. We both cried. Cricket had been Caroline's very first pony, the first foray our family took into the horse world that now occupies so much of our time. Cricket guided Caroline through her first 4-H shows and county fairs and brought home the first ribbons to adorn her now-covered walls.

Her age was never certain. The hand-lettered sign on a country road near our house said, "16-year-old pony for sale." We visited the barn and found a sweet-faced brownish-gray pony with a white blaze. "Half POA and half Welsh," the sellers told us. With a minimal investment and even less knowledge, we signed the check and walked our ecstatic daughter home on her very own pony.

We called the vet for an initial checkup and whatever shots were needed. She laughed out loud when we told her the pony was sixteen. "*All* old ponies are 'sixteen' when they're for sale!" she said, wryly. She rubbed her hands over a slightly knobby knee, peered into the mouth. "Nope," she declared. "Hard to tell for sure, but this girl's at least twenty. She's in good shape, though, a nice little mare." She patted her approvingly. "She's a fine beginner's mount for a lightweight like your daughter."

I'm still not sure if she was just breaking it to us gently, or if she was genuinely unsure of Cricket's age, but each time Dr. Lisa came back for the spring or fall checkup, she'd add another five years. Shaking her head, she'd say, "She's at *least* twenty-five." Then, six months later, "No, she's got to be over thirty!" Finally, examining teeth that were worn almost to the gum line, she wouldn't even hazard any more guesses. When asked what she thought was Cricket's age, "She's ancient!" was all she'd say.

As our equine experience grew, we appreciated more how purely lucky we were to adopt Cricket. She had almost none of the bad habits or grumpiness that old ponies are notorious for and the smaller or more timid a rider we put on her back, the calmer and steadier she became. But with Caroline's increasing riding skills, Cricket would perk up and show off with the jauntiest little jog in the arena. That pony could high-step merrily over fallen and crossed logs on the trail course that all the "real" horses knocked and stumbled over.

At the first horse show of our lives, Caroline saddled up and Cricket calmly walked to the pole, stepped two dainty front hooves over and side-passed its length, elegant as any ballerina. Our 4-H leader, uncharacteristically wordless, just stared openmouthed as Caroline successfully navigated a difficult course and rode home with a blue ribbon.

When Caroline's adolescent legs sprouted so that she was suddenly able to cross her ankles under Cricket's belly (well, almost), she graduated to a Quarter Horse, but Cricket stayed on, part of the family. Young friends visited for pony rides and simple lessons. Caroline theoretically gave the lessons, but Cricket did the teaching. And she served well as an amateur therapy pony, offering rides and confidence to countless toddlers and preschoolers with disabilities who were my students. But eventually, she grew too slow and stiff for even their small bodies and gentle demands. More finicky as she aged, she turned her nose up at the high-calorie grain-mashes and supplements with which we tried to build up her weight; getting medicine into her in any form was virtually impossible.

That dreary, early spring day when Caroline found Cricket unmoving in the cold, we knew the time was coming. We gave ourselves a day or two to make the decision, postponing the inevitable. But then, the weather turned and spring arrived. Warm sunny days soothed Cricket's aches and pains and we didn't find her lying down again. She even trotted and galloped a few times, keeping up with the bigger horses in her pasture as they raced about full of spring fever, and she gained a few pounds on the lush spring grass.

Now, the summer reprieve is over. Wet leaves clutter the roadsides, fog covers the river each morning and a chill sweeps down from the mountains to the east. Cricket moves more slowly each day, not venturing far in the open pasture. Knees big as baseballs, she can barely bend a leg. The weight she added in the early summer has slipped away, leaving bony ribs under thickening fur.

It really is time to say good-bye. I schedule the farm call with the receptionist. "But please have Lisa give me a call," I add. I've barely hung up before uncertainty creeps back. Should we really do this? Cricket was standing, contentedly basking in her sunny pasture when I checked on her. Is it right to end her life, am I just doing it for my own convenience? But I remember the gaunt feel of her sharp haunches. I don't want to wait until she is once more lying in a cold rain, unable to move.

Lisa calls, with her gentle manner. I tell her my qualms; she empathizes and assures me I can change my mind before the appointment. "It has to feel right to you," she says. I remember that with at least two previous pets, elderly dogs, I harbored these same doubts, only to worry about the flip side after each was finally buried: *Did I wait too long? Did he suffer too much before the end?* It is often a case of guesswork. Life or death guesswork.

We give Caroline the option of being present at the euthanizing or not. She is adamant—she will be there to say good-bye.

Trustingly, Cricket follows her girl, hardly needing a lead rope. A last kiss on a velvety muzzle, then the swift injection. Cricket's head drops, her knees bend as if she is beginning to lie herself down, then the old body folds heavily to the ground. She is gone, mercifully, before the collapse is complete.

We have been through this with dogs and cats before, but still are not prepared for the rush of grief. Caroline and I cling together as sobs and tears gush up; we thought we were ready, but . . . oh! Cricket! My pony!

But, as the old hymn says, "It is well with my soul." It was time. Inwardly, I thank this old friend for bringing joy to our lives and trusting us to care for her until the very end.

Barbara S. Greenstreet

Mr. Feelin' Good

Life is too short to be little.

Benjamin Disraeli

He was nineteen when he came into my life. Long past his prime. I was hesitant to make the investment but Charlie assured me he had one more season left in him. "He'll teach you a lot about showing reining horses," Charlie explained, "You're getting a $20,000 horse for one tenth the money." A consummate salesman, Charlie had always been a horse trader with the ability to make a person feel like if they said no they'd just lost out on a good thing. He knew this horse better than anyone; he'd bought and sold him many times over the years. I knew he was giving me an opportunity, so we closed the deal and I loaded the old gelding into my trailer, a simple stock type made of steel pipe.

It was a twelve-hour haul from Charlie's place to my home in Florida. I checked my side mirror regularly during the trip. A nose poking out through the bars periodically would let me know the horse was still on his feet and breathing. I worried about the old guy the whole way home but when we finally pulled up in front of my barn and I opened up the trailer I soon discovered my worries were unfounded. The big sorrel gelding peered out at me with bright eyes. He stepped out boldly, ears up, snorting and shaking his head. *This is a horse that lives up to his name,* I observed with a smile, *He really is Mr. Feelin' Good!*

Sixteen years had passed since Mr. Feelin' Good (FG) had lived in Florida. Bred in Ocala he was now home again. I turned him out in the paddock and watched in amazement as FG took off running and bucking. It certainly wasn't difficult to picture the fresh young three-year-old futurity prospect he once had been. These days the gray was beginning to show around his face and nearly two decades of steady competition had left its mark on his body. But one look into his large brown eyes revealed a spirit that was vibrant and unbroken. The depth of his powerful energy was evident from the first time I stepped up on him. It coursed up through his feet, pounded through his enormous heart, then patiently waited for release in the draped reins I held between the thumb and fingers of my left hand. This was a highly trained performance horse, the product of years of refinement. I hoped I was up for the challenge. As it turned out, FG would show me much more than just how to ride better, he would teach me about life itself.

My show career had been pretty dismal before FG came along. So you can imagine my surprise when I entered my first reining with him and won! Charlie was sure right about this old guy. FG was a terrific horse to show. Overnight he transformed me from an also-ran to a contender. Reining is a demanding sport for both the horse and the rider. It's an event that is designed to demonstrate the speed, agility and athleticism of the Western stock horse. Riders enter the show ring alone and must perform from memory one of ten different patterns. Each pattern is a combination of seven different reining maneuvers. The most famous of these are the sliding stop and the spin. FG was great at spinning but his real talent was in his enormous stops. It was not uncommon for him to slide forty feet before finally coming to rest.

It didn't take long to realize I was riding a celebrity. Every show ground I took him to, people would recognize old FG. I called the National Reining Horse Association to request his show record and was amazed when my fax machine yielded nine pages of data. Scanning the lists of venues it seemed as if he'd competed in nearly every part of the United States and Canada. Many people had owned him over the years, most only for a season or two, but all of them winners. With Mr. Feelin' Good as their dancing partner, they'd gone to the finals at the NRHA Futurity and the NRHA Derby, won multiple NRHA Affiliate championships, dozens of bronze trophies, and even a world title.

As the show season progressed, my own win record grew as did my desire to keep winning. Through it all FG never complained; like a faithful blue-collar worker, he punched his time card into the company clock everyday and went to work. Slowly, subtly, I began to change. I was no longer surprised when I won at a show, I was expecting it. Charlie had warned me about this, he'd told me that everyone who showed FG eventually got a big head. I'd listened, but I really hadn't heard the words. I would come to understand that although competition is meant to bring out the best in us, it can just as easily bring out the worst.

FG is one of those rare horses who never mellowed with age. His huge heart seemed to drive an endless supply of energy that transcended any physical limitation. He was always at the ready, always so reliable. And like so many years before, it was shaping up to be yet another winning show season. It's an intoxicating feeling to enter a class knowing you can win it. The more I won the more I wanted to keep winning. But what I couldn't see was, despite his tremendous drive, it was becoming increasingly more difficult for FG's body to keep up the pace. I took him to a specialist and had his joints injected, I gave him regular shots of drugs to keep him sound and before every show, I put pain killers in his feed. One night I was leading FG back through the barns after a class. Two men passed me in the alleyway and I overheard one say to the other, "That horse'll be dead soon." The words chilled me to my core.

A good friend and mentor of mine once told me that there is no forgiveness like the forgiveness in a horse. I was so blinded by my desire to win, I couldn't see how increasingly painful it was for FG every time I took him into the arena and yet, in spite of his pain, FG kept trying for me. There are many obvious ways to abuse our horses. It's the subtle abuses that sneak up on us. FG was lucky; I woke up before it was too late. Soon after that night in the show barn, I had my blacksmith remove FG's slide plates for the last time.

In 1998 Mr. Feelin' Good was inducted into the National Reining Horse Association's Hall of Fame. Today, at twenty-seven, you'll find him living a quite retirement at our ranch in Ocala, just a few miles from the place he was born, grazing in a green pasture among shady oaks. He still runs and bucks in his paddock and enjoys an occasional trail ride for a change of scenery.

Tracy Schumer

The String

In the depth of winter I finally learned there was in me invincible summer.

Albert Camus

As a researcher and horsemanship instructor, I've met many people from all over the world, most with two things in common: a love of horses and a strong desire to improve in whatever they want to do with them. Some years ago, Barbara, a fortyish woman from Germany attended one of our programs at the Equine Research Foundation (ERF). The non-profit Foundation, which I run with my partner, Jerry Ingersoll, is dedicated to advancing knowledge about equine cognition, perception and behavior and improving the human/horse relationship as well as the care and well-being of horses. People from all walks of life come to the Foundation for learning and riding vacations of one or two weeks with internships ranging from one to three months.

Barbara had worked in jobs that required quite a bit of social interaction. Curious about cognition and social behavior, she was eager to learn more about learning abilities and how behaviorism played into everyday interactions between people and their animals. She arrived without much knowledge about horses or research but enthusiasm enough to make up for it.

For half of every day, Barbara and other volunteers assisted with our research. The rest of the time, she was immersed in hands-on horseplay where participants learned about and honed their skills in horse handling, training and bonding using ERF techniques. Not everything came easily to Barbara. Horse handling at the Foundation was new and different from what she had come across in her occasional ride in a formal venue. The straightforward part was learning how to assist with the research. Data on how horses perceive their world and how they assimilate what they encounter grew daily. Everyone was excited to learn that horses could generalize and form categories and, even more astonishingly, use some degree of conceptualization. This was groundbreaking research and we all had worked together to make it happen.

Real challenges came when participants were asked to develop a positive relationship, a real partnership, with the horses. Those who ride only rental or lesson horses are not generally given the chance to bond with their horses and even some horse owners miss out on this valuable and rewarding opportunity. Riders are shown the correct hand and leg signals needed for directing a horse but are taught little about how to develop a relationship that makes the horse want to be with them, anytime, anywhere. Thus, they rarely have the occasion to communicate with horses as horses do with one another, which is the foundation of true horsemanship.

Barbara and the other participants watched as our horses followed and hung out with Jerry and myself at liberty, without halter, lead rope, or any other kind of tack. They speculated on what would motivate horses to leave their food or herd mates to be with us. They pondered over why it all looked so simple when we did it and how we always seemed to know what would happen next. They sure didn't believe that within a week or so they, too, would possess the knowledge and skills to do the same. And they looked at us kind of funny when we asked what the strongest lead rope was made out of.

Eager, hopeful, yet doubting her abilities, Barbara began working with our horses. When she walked toward them, they walked off. When she asked them to move left, they moved right. When she tried to raise their heads for haltering, they continued grazing. When all else failed, sweet-talk also failed. Discouraged and humbled, Barbara lamented that she'd never catch on and that the horses responded to her the same way some people did. Although she worked hard at her job back home, she felt she wasn't communicating with her colleagues effectively. Distressing parallels between her interactions with horses and her relationships with people became evident to her. Something had to change.

Days at ERF went by with Barbara engrossed in horse cognition and behavior. She noted how we based our interactions on equine social behavior—treating our horses as they would each other—and how we used positive reinforcement frequently. Within the first week, Barbara was feeling good about herself. She could get the horses to do as she asked under saddle and they would follow her nicely on the ground, at least on a lead rope. Now it was time for one more challenge.

One morning during the second week of her stay, I asked Barbara to go out and bring in our Paint gelding, Coco Bean, a spirited two-year-old with a mind of his own. No pushover, he could instantly read the abilities of any human and would treat them accordingly. Barbara had worked with Coco Bean a bit in days previous and felt fairly confident about heading out to catch him, halter and twelve-foot lead rope in hand.

She was halfway out the stable door when I asked, "What's that in your hand?"

"Why, it's a halter and lead rope." Barbara replied.

"What do you need that for?" I asked.

Barbara looked at me as if I was daft and answered, "To put on the horse to bring him in."

"Oh. Well, wait a minute." I walked into the tack room and returned dangling an eight-inch piece of cotton string and said, "Use this instead."

"Instead of what?" Barbara said, alarmed.

"Leave the halter and lead rope here and bring Coco Bean in with just this string." I said.

Barbara laughed nervously, "Yeah, right, you expect me to bring in a 1,000 pound horse with this fragment of string?"

"Yep," I answered with a smile.

"I can't do that," Barbara fretted, "It's impossible!"

"I think you might be able to," I answered. Muttering something in German and shaking her head, Barbara reluctantly took the string and headed out, anticipating defeat.

We watched from the fence as she approached Coco Bean. Coco gave her an assessing look and wavered between standing still and leaving. As Barbara neared him, he took a few steps in the opposite direction. Without the security of the halter and lead rope, Barbara reverted to her old ways, anxiously calling Coco while trying to head him off. Coco Bean, recognizing her lack of confidence, reacted instinctively and trotted off. I heard a collective groan from the other participants but kept an eye on Barbara. It was exactly at that moment that it all clicked. Her body posture changed, as did her demeanor. She relaxed. She became confident. What she had learned about horse behavior and training during the days at the ERF kicked in and she became a leader.

String in hand but not even in use, she approached Coco Bean, drawing only on her newly acquired body language to ask him to turn and face her. When he did, she casually turned and walked off. It was a moment to remember, watching her exultant face as she strolled all over the two-acre pasture, untethered horse following her every footstep. She had just discovered that the strongest lead rope was the invisible one—the bond between horse and human.

Barbara returned to Germany and Jerry and I continued our work at ERF. On a spring day years later, I was in the stable running a new experiment when I heard voices outside. I stuck my head out the door and there was Barbara. As we walked around, Barbara exclaimed at all of the changes we had made, including the addition of six more horses. While standing by them, Barbara suddenly said, "I have something to show you." She lifted her shirt a little and pointed to her belt loop. Tied to it was a ragged eight-inch piece of string. I looked at her with a puzzled expression and she said, "Remember this? I keep it with me always. It's my symbol to tell me that I am capable of accomplishing anything."

Evelyn B. Hanggi, M.S., Ph.D.

A Bridge Beyond

I am not a phoenix yet, but here among the ashes, it may be that the pain is chiefly that of new wings trying to push through.

May Sarton

Feeling giddy like three green buckaroos on their first day of a cattle drive, my two children and I were standing next to the pasture gate waiting to meet Dodger for the first time. Weeks earlier, my husband and I had purchased this Mustang based only on his description. The ranch owner was sure that the fifteen-year-old Mustang, who had been "gathered" by the Bureau of Land Management eleven years earlier, would work out well for us. When my ten-year-old son Daniel heard that the new horse was a Mustang, he made his intentions clear. The new horse had to belong to him.

Many things in Daniel's short life have presented challenges. Because he is autistic, what others take for granted Daniel struggles to achieve or simply abandons. Just a few months prior, a lesson horse ran away with Daniel at a full gallop during one of his earliest riding lessons. He suffered little physical injury in spite of being hurled into the pipe corral fencing at the arena. The injuries to his confidence, however, were devastating.

Something about the possibility of having a Mustang as his own pony rekindled a spark, a seemingly dead ember, in Daniel's heart. Little did I know this match was more than the romanticized whim of a ten-year-old boy. If their introductory meeting was any indication, Dodger had similar designs on Daniel.

Observing the newest member of our family from a distance, Dodger's posture was reminiscent of bygone days of the Wild West and the struggle for survival. Our sorrel gelding stood rigid, tense and wide-eyed. The owner explained that this horse was unwilling for a human to approach and halter him without the benefit of a grain bucket. The carrots we had so eagerly brought with us would be wasted, he explained, as Dodger wouldn't take food from any human's hand. Surely, this wasn't a horse that would be right for our family? How can a horse with "issues" possibly be a good match for a boy like our Daniel?

As the adults droned on, not privy to the warnings given by Dodger's owner, Daniel silently slipped out to the pasture, halter in hand, introduced himself to his new friend and triumphantly led him over to meet us. Later that day, Dodger relished a carrot Daniel offered to him. An unlikely bridge was forming, linking the world of a formerly abused Mustang pony with that of a socially challenged ten-year-old boy.

Dodger came home to us a month later. As we worked with him, we noticed that he drew inside of himself. It was clear that his survival mechanisms included disassociating, most likely due to the harsh handling he had previously experienced. Occasionally, as if to confirm the story told by his physical scars, Dodger would tremble seemingly convinced he would be beaten or even killed.

Early on, only Daniel could approach Dodger without causing this emotional shut down. Dodger welcomed Daniel into his world with utter abandon. Content to brush his pony or to tenderly care for his hoofs without the benefits of halter and lead rope, the two partners enjoyed one another's company down in the pasture. Sometimes, Dodger followed Daniel around the forested hillside pasture seeming to refuse to let go of the comfort and camaraderie he garnered from the presence of his special boy.

Dodger trusted humans again, a little at a time. Because of this Mustang, Daniel began to see that he had something special to offer others. The little pony with intuition and insight quickly won a place in our hearts and our home forever.

Recently, just after school let out for summer break, Daniel made the rare announcement that he would like to ride. Still not eager to venture beyond the corral at home, Daniel trusts only Dodger to carry him. On a mild June morning, we headed down to the pasture where Dodger's shrill whinny greeted us. Poking over the gate to welcome us in a wet nuzzle, Dodger's Roman nose slopes nobly downward to a severe and sudden indentation, irrefutable evidence of the handling he received in the past. The physical scars on both sides of our Mustang's face betray the truth about his previous life. But in spite of what came before, he stood at the gate eager to give the gift of himself, a priceless treasure. The significance of this is never lost on us.

Helmeted and ready to ride, my son haltered his equine friend as he had many times in the previous two and a half years. Content with the halter and a loop rein as their only tack, they prefer riding bareback to the constraints of a saddle. Realizing that I left the clip-on rein up at the trailer, I assured Daniel I would be right back with the reins so he could ride. A minute or two later I came down the hill toward the corral and spied Daniel sitting astride Dodger, negotiating serpentines, figure eights and circles in the corral just like pros—with only a lead rope in one of Daniel's hands attached to his partner's halter. Daniel grinned ear-to-ear as the two of them promenaded around the corral, as a true natural horseman and his partner should.

Moments spent forging the bond between horse and boy were too precious to waste waiting for my return. Daniel had climbed on to the feeding trough (our makeshift mounting block) and Dodger had sided-up, inviting Daniel to join him for a ride. Unwilling to refuse so gracious an invitation, my son had hopped aboard.

The lightness and softness with which Dodger now responded to Daniel's un-schooled cues took my breath away. Together they had found a safe place for both of them. Daniel and Dodger's ride lasted perhaps ten minutes, but the effects continue to defy all the confidence-shaking experiences each of them endured before their paths joined.

Daniel violated an immutable rule in our home—that no one mounts a horse without an adult present. But given that there was a larger, more absolute law overriding any rules that I might attempt to instill, I chose not to rebuke him. All things had come together in an instant: Daniel's confidence, the invitation of his pony, even the helmet perched upon Daniel's head. It was a moment like the day we first met Dodger—a moment that was meant to be.

Having journeyed a great distance to be such a willing, solicitous partner to a young autistic boy, Dodger has carried all of us so far. Because of this unique Mustang, my son changed forever, infused with a confidence provided only by a special relationship of which so many of us who love horses can only dream.

Heidi Bylsma

Hero of the Week

Great opportunities to help others seldom come, but small ones surround us every day.

Sally Koch

The telephone rang just as I was settling the kids down for the evening. When I heard the voice of Sgt. Scott Cataldi, a boarder in our barn and a local police officer, on the other end of the line I listened with concern. In one quick breath, he said, "There's a horse in tough shape and we need your help. It's bad." I took the directions, dropped everything, left the kids with my husband and flew out the door.

I had never seen any sign of life, let alone a horse, at the small, nondescript tract house I had passed many times. My stomach churned as I got out of the car to meet Scott. He introduced me to his fellow officer, Gay Weyland, and Peggy Drummey, a local horse owner who had also volunteered to help. As we walked past the "For Sale" sign in the front yard, the officers explained that a house painter had called the station after he heard noises in a shed while preparing an estimate for a job. So upset by what he found, he begged the officers to investigate immediately.

Dodging overgrown thistles and brambles, we gingerly

made our way through the weeds and trash to the small, dilapidated shack in the back yard. It was inconceivable that an animal could possibly be alive in that cramped, foul smelling shed. The stench of manure and ammonia hit us long before we reached the door. Pushing it open we could see only a dark, dingy area with a yellow slash of early evening light coming through a small window the color of old wax paper. Dirty metal trash cans sat empty in the corner except for a dusty collection of spiders and dead mice. The floor was littered with crumpled plastic bread bags and there was no grain, no hay, no sign of life.

Suddenly, from my left there came a slight blowing sound, like a soft whisper. We turned and saw two soft brown eyes peering down at us through a haze of cobwebs. We wrestled open the door of the stall to find a small chestnut horse standing above us on layers of manure so thick he couldn't raise his head without hitting it on the rafters. He turned toward us but didn't move and we realized with horror that his tail, which was embedded six inches in a solid block of concrete-like manure, rooted him to the ground. His hooves curled up through the dank, viscous mixture like thick Turkish slippers and everywhere he could reach the wooden planks of his prison, he had eaten them down to splinters in a last ditch effort to survive.

"Easy boy," said Officer Cataldi. Blinking back tears, I stepped up into the stall with him to assess just how bad it was. Gently turning his head he nickered to us again, a soft velvety sound that came from deep within his chest, followed by a short grunt of exhaustion. He blinked his eyes, squinted in the beam of the flashlight and waited for us to help him. As my eyes passed over his pathetic frame, I could not believe a horse could be so filthy, emaciated and alive.

It was clear he could not stay in such filthy conditions, but his hooves were so deformed and he had been forced to stand in the same position for so long, he could barely move. As we were considering the various options, Peggy suddenly gasped, "My God, I know this horse. It can't be. I haven't seen him in years but he is Master MacDuff and I know him from local horse shows a few years ago. Duffy was a champion and a gorgeous Morab," she said with a sigh, shaking her head in disgust.

We decided that the safest place for Duffy would be my farm, a few miles away. There, we could make a better assessment of his condition and get veterinary help while the police pursued the case against his owner. I hadn't lived here long, knew few people in town and had never met Duffy's owner so my farm was a good, safe option.

After cutting off the hunk of tail hair embedded in manure, we encouraged him to move, step-by-step with our arms around and under him as we gently turned and lowered him down, actually carrying him out of his manure encrusted prison. Duffy surprised us by stepping carefully but deliberately onto the trailer, as if he knew we were there to help him. It was heartbreaking to watch him move, stumbling over his deformed hooves and I was struck by the fact that instead of hating humans after all he had been through, he welcomed us and willingly gave us his trust.

When he stepped into the light of our stable yard, we were able to take in the full measure of his emaciated condition. His dull chestnut coat was a patchwork of mats, burrs, sores and manure and his legs were thick with fluid in sharp contrast to his emaciated body. His tail was a tornado shaped tangle of twisted knots, manure and sticks embedded in manure. Beneath the mottled dull coat, Duffy's bones strained against his skin in every direction. Sores oozed where brambles had worked their way to his skin and his hooves reeked of thrush.

We gave him small sips of water, careful not to give him too much and I prepared a small, watery bran mash for him. We were thrilled when he showed a slight interest in it, but we shared a grave concern about his chances for survival after such an ordeal. After Peggy and the officers left, I began treating Duffy's sores and cutting the mats out of his fur.

The police officers returned the next morning with a

veterinarian to document Duffy's condition. "He is almost 300 pounds under normal body weight, he has extreme malnutrition, dehydration and he is very close to torpor, the last stage the body goes through as it basically feeds off itself before shutting down. But he is tough to have made it this far," said Dr. Tusch, shaking his head. Donna Rand, a local farrier, donated her services and carefully trimmed back Duffy's overgrown hooves, giving him more freedom to move.

It was a quiet, slow, steady climb back to life on the privacy of our farm. Day by day, we noticed small improvements in Duffy's condition. At first he accepted our attention with a bland sort of indifference, but on the fourth morning Duffy surprised me by greeting me with an enthusiastic whinny and I knew he was going to survive. When Duffy was strong enough to endure the trailer ride, he continued his long road to recovery at the Maine State Society for the Protection of Animals until his ultimate fate was decided in the courts. It was heartbreaking to let him go, but I knew he would be in good hands.

Duffy's owner was successfully prosecuted and Duffy became the property of the State of Maine. Despite offers for adoption, Duffy had become such a beloved member of the MSSPA community they decided to keep him as their mascot. When a local television station profiled his will to survive and proclaimed Duffy "Hero of the Week," donations poured into animal rescue organizations throughout the state in Duffy's name.

Duffy's determination to survive against such long odds continued to inspire everyone who heard his story. House painter Don Chasse, who didn't look the other way when he came upon Duffy in the shed; Officers Cataldi and Weyland who took the matter seriously, ultimately saving Duffy's life and I am honored to have helped him in a small way. He lived out the rest of his days at the MSSPA surrounded by loving caretakers and equine friends.

Susan Winslow

3

HORSES AS HEALERS

There is something about jumping a horse over a fence, something that makes you feel good. Perhaps it's the risk, the gamble. In any event it's a thing I need.

William Faulkner

Gracie

*Success is to be measured not so much by the
position that one has reached in life as by the
obstacles, which he has overcome while trying to
succeed.*

Booker T. Washington

"Dr. Wendy, I really need your advice . . ." Ralph's voice
quivered. He and his wife, Teresa, lived several hours north of
the mixed animal veterinary hospital my husband, Bryant,
and I had started from scratch six years earlier. The reason for
his call today was the plight of his beloved mare, Lady. Lady
was an older bay racking mare that he had bred to a nice black
and white Walking Horse stallion the previous year. Lady had
developed a severe cancer in her mouth and he did not expect
her to live long enough to carry her foal to term. I was
uniquely qualified to help him, not only because of my veterinary expertise.

At the age of thirty-one, my discovery of an unusual lump
in one of my breasts was a devastating introduction to cancer.
I underwent a double mastectomy, six months of chemotherapy and took Tamoxifen for several years. I was a cancer
"survivor" but I truly felt like a "victim." Bryant and I had been

married five years and were talking about starting a family when the appearance of the lump changed our plans. After treatment I still had a strong desire to start a family but I struggled with the "what ifs" that I was facing. What if I got pregnant and my cancer returned? What decisions would I have to make concerning my baby and my treatment options? What if I died? Who would take care of my child? Would he or she experience enough love without their real mother?

One Sunday afternoon in April of 2002, a home pregnancy test left me stunned as I watched an unmistakable double line appear. It is the rare moment in life when abject fear blends with incredible jubilation. I wasn't sure how to handle that moment. I turned on the shower and let the hot water wash over me, stifling my sobs and taking my tears down the drain.

A little over a week later Ralph brought Lady into our clinic to follow through with the plan we had devised. Lady's cancer had indeed progressed quickly and although Ralph had given her the very best of care, he was no longer able to help her stay comfortable. Lady had given up and it was evident in the distant gaze of her eyes and the solemn droop to her once-proud head. Although she was past her due date, we had no idea how developed the foal would be considering the stressed state Lady's body had been in for many months. I said my good-byes to Lady as Bryant and Ralph were in the clinic getting things ready. She stood weakly in the iron stocks of our horse barn as I cradled her head in my hands, trying to avoid the ghastly tumor that was coming out of her jaw like a large melon. Blood and liquid gruel drained from the corners of her mouth.

She was one of the first to learn that I was pregnant. I revealed my own fears as my tears mixed with her blood and dropped to the barn floor. I told her that I was going to be a mother myself, that my only wish was for my child to be healthy and happy and to have plenty of love and attention. I promised her that I would help make sure her foal got the best of care and that I would mother it as best I could while it was here. For a moment, human and horse were uniquely connected by the bonds of both cancer and motherhood. And for a moment, I prayed that Lady would understand and would be at peace.

As the sun set that evening, Bryant quickly and expertly performed the C-section and laid a perfectly marked black and white filly onto the blankets next to Lady. The tiny form of a horse that looked like she wasn't ready for the real world yet struck me. Still, she was beautiful. Her tiny ears curved up and the tips touched, forming a little heart halo above her head. Ralph and I dried her off and stimulated her chest trying to turn her tiny gasps into deep healthy breaths. I didn't watch as Bryant injected Lady and laid her to rest. I concentrated instead on my promise to save her foal. Several hours later, Ralph and his father sadly drove away with Lady's lifeless body in the back of their trailer.

The filly was alive, but barely. We laid her on thick comforters against a bale of straw and put a blanket on top of her. Warm intravenous fluids flowed into her jugular vein and a heat lamp sent a rosy glow over the stall. One of the barn cats kept me company that night, sitting on the hay bale perched over the filly, while I lay on a blanket on the stall floor next to her. The filly was weak and slipped in and out of consciousness. I felt silly telling her to be a fighter . . . telling her about her mother and about all the trouble Ralph had gone through for her. I didn't sleep much that night but I remember hearing her first throaty nicker as I drifted into one nap, thinking what a beautiful sound that was.

For the next few days, I alternated between caring for the filly and reporting her progress to Ralph and his family and to the Internet group on a popular gaited-horse forum where Lady's story was well known. The filly grew strong enough to sit up and stand with assistance. We fed her foal milk through a feeding tube every few hours and kept her on every drug and supplement we knew of to keep her healthy and strong. Either Bryant or I—or both—slept in the stall with her. During this time, Bryant and I would talk for hours. I revealed to him at one point that if our baby was a girl, I wanted to name her Grace, because it was only through the Grace of God that I had survived my cancer and was pregnant.

The next day, Ralph and Teresa came down to check on the filly. They knelt by her side as Ralph told me that they had picked out a name for her. "Grace," they both said at once. Through misty eyes, I told them that Bryant and I had recently found out that I was carrying a baby and that we had decided to name it the same thing if it was a girl. My connection to the little filly grew even deeper.

Gracie was seldom alone in her stall. When she was three-weeks-old, she was drinking well from a bottle and we felt like she was strong enough to go home. Less than forty-eight hours later, poor Gracie was back in our clinic. Ralph and his family had spent most of each day and night with her, but the stress of the trip had given her pneumonia. She was very sick. Morale in the clinic, on the gaited-horse forum and in Ralph's household was at its lowest. I felt like I had failed Ralph, Gracie and Lady.

We started from the bottom again, putting Grace on intravenous fluids and medications and tube-feeding her. Morning sickness crept into my life about that same time, eerily similar to the nausea that chemotherapy brought on years earlier. I sat next to Grace, stroking her silky curved ears and giving her—and myself—pep talks about being a fighter. I told her about all the support and love she had, as if a tiny filly would understand any of that.

Grace slowly responded and over the next week rebounded. It wasn't long before Ralph was able to take her home again . . . this time to a Thoroughbred nurse-mare he had lined up. Unfortunately, the mare would allow Grace to nurse only if several people restrained her and Ralph feared the mare would injure Grace if the two were alone together. Just when all hope seemed lost, Ralph recalled an e-mail he had seen shortly after Gracie was born. A farm manager's wife had offered the services of one of many soon-to-be-weaned Rocky Mountain Horse farm mares. In desperation and exhausted from bottle-feeding Grace at all hours, Ralph contacted the farm and was elated to hear the offer still stood. Gracie's new mom was a gorgeous, large buckskin mare named Dolly. They allowed Dolly's colt to nurse one last time, then led him away and introduced Gracie. Ralph says it was a magical moment when they realized the new pairing was going to be successful. Gracie took several long drinks of precious real milk from a real mom and the pair were loaded back up onto Ralph's trailer and taken home. Dolly nickered and talked to Gracie the entire ride and by the time they got home, they were inseparable.

Several weeks later, Bryant and I drove to Ralph's house to see the pair in person. At the sound of Ralph's voice, Gracie tore around the corner of the barn to the fence where we were standing. Dolly followed in panicked pursuit, not wanting her filly to get too far from her side. As Dolly came up to us, she nickered and nudged Gracie with her muzzle, with all the love a mother has for a child. It melted my heart. As Gracie turned and hunted for Dolly's milk, I drew a large sigh. Lady would be so happy at this scene . . . her foal was well taken care of and well loved. I instinctively put my hand on my growing belly and smiled.

Bryant Jr.—Bart—was born five months later. I remain healthy and as I write this, Alex is growing inside me. If something should happen to me, I no longer worry about the "what ifs." I know both boys will be raised surrounded by love and attention. Meanwhile, Gracie is a gorgeous three-year-old celebrity. She has been shown in halter and under saddle and Ralph enlists her help every year for the local Heart Association "filly bingo." Everywhere she goes, she attracts attention. Her pretty ears remain curled inward and her gorgeous velvety coat glows with health. I will always remain indebted to this special filly. She showed me that despite the darkness of cancer, the circle of life flourishes.

Wendy Wade Morton, D.V.M.

A Mustang Night

Being deeply loved by someone gives you strength; loving someone deeply gives you courage.

Lao-tzu

A dull ache in her lower back awoke my grandma Violet one gray dawn in July of 1931. She lay quietly, listening to grandpa's breathing next to her, wondering exactly what this pain was that she was feeling. She was sixteen years old then, grandpa George was eighteen and they were expecting their first baby. Thoughts of me were far in the future. They were living in grandma's parents' house in Melrose, Idaho, because Vi still needed her mama and daddy and it was the Depression. Life was hard in spite of their love for each other. A man worked all week for one sack of spuds, while the women worked just as hard trying to grow a garden, washing the clothes by hand, keeping the house up and raising all the kids.

Another ache, this one a little stronger, brought Vi back to the present. She turned on her side and brushed George's arm softly. "Mornin," she whispered to him, watching as his eyes squinted first, then opened slowly.

"Hmmm," he groaned.

"I think today might be it," she said as she moved closer to his ear.

He immediately turned to her and smiled, then placed his large hand over her stomach, like he'd done so many times to feel the little feet and hands flutter. "Does it hurt? Do you want me to stay home?"

She thought for a minute. "No. Mama's here and who knows when it'll be. It's best if you just go on to work with Daddy."

George pulled on his worn boots to go out and do chores before breakfast. "I still need to break that horse your dad gave me," he said almost every morning before he went out the door, this morning no exception. By the time he got home every night he was too tired to tend to the dun Mustang that decorated the pen outside their window with his gallant flaxen mane and tail. Before he'd moved up to Idaho, George broke horses for other people and before he married Violet, he'd told his father-in-law he missed that. When Erastus surprised him with the stallion as a wedding gift, George was speechless.

The three-year-old stallion they had named Dusty was unpredictable. Even though he looked gentle and would come up to the fence to be petted or to get a carrot, once you got inside the pen with him you'd better look out. This morning, as the sun began to break up over the distant mountains, George sensed an urgent restlessness in the horse. His neck arched, Dusty pranced around the pen, front legs high and quick and anxious. He looked at the worn leather tack that had traveled with him from California and walked over to feel the cracks beneath his calloused fingers. It was as if the stallion were taunting him, inviting him to take on the challenge and it was all George could do to turn around and walk back in the house.

At work his mind wandered first to Vi and the baby, then to the Mustang that had beckoned him that morning. Something distant and wild and disturbing pricked at his mind all day—something that he struggled to make sense of and hold on to. It was the Great Depression and grandpa George had no way of seeing into the future. All he felt was the harsh reality of the here and now and a weight of life that threatened to suffocate him. What scared him more than anything though, was his inability to tell Vi how he felt.

While George was at work, grandma Vi's labor pains grew more intense every hour. She kept working until the pain finally dropped her onto the bed and by the time George arrived at home that evening, she was in the final hours before delivery. With her mother anxiously by her side, coaching her and soothing her, Violet finally pushed the little boy into her mother's hands and wouldn't lay back until she heard him cry. But the cry was weak and great-grandma knew it. She wiped the boy clean and wrapped him tightly in a square of cotton, then handed her first grandson gently to Vi.

Grandpa was rushed into the room and the two named my small uncle Don George Lundvall. After he died later that night, grandma grew silent and George wrapped himself up even more in his work. Every day he walked by the corral trying not to look at the Mustang. Grandma Vi went about her chores systematically, trying to understand this new sense of self that had blossomed and suddenly died with her son's last breath.

On the evening of the thirty-first day after his baby died and his wife quit talking to him, George walked out of the quiet house and straight to the barn where he grabbed the worn saddle and threw it up over the top rail of the corral fence. The Mustang snorted and backed away from the saddle, then spun on its haunches and ran straight to the corner, quivering.

"Whoa, boy." George's soothing voice echoed from the barn as he brushed the dust and hay from the saddle blanket. Then he walked to the garden and pulled two young carrots, stuffing one in his shirt pocket, snapping it shut and holding the other out for the Mustang as he unlatched the gate and walked to the corner of the pen.

The Mustang must have sensed George's determination and decided to meet it head-on. Although he accepted the halter easily enough, that was the only part of the night that would be easy. The battle raged long into the night. Great-grandpa Erastus walked out to the corral several times to bring water and to tell George to call it a night—to let the horse be for now. But George wouldn't have it. The pain felt too good.

George needed to be beaten as much as he needed to win. He needed to hurt physically and to have a reason to scream and to let his tears flow where no one could see. He knew that the Mustang understood him like no one else did. Grandpa knew that horses, with their incredible sixth sense, were the best therapy in life.

Inside the house, Vi finally couldn't resist going to the window to watch. She'd listened to her siblings as they'd run in and out of the house, screaming, "Whoa, did you see that?" too many times. As she watched her husband from the window, with each blow and each fall, she cried harder for George. Slowly she began to understand what she'd done by shutting him out. She knew that she would never be the same again, but watching George and Dusty through the pane glass window planted something new in her soul—some kind of hope. She began to plan what she would say to George the next morning.

Just as the Milky Way erupted in the night sky, the Mustang finally gave in. As the dust from the pen rose up into the wind and dissipated into the night sky, so the conflicts of the stallion and my grandpa mingled and disappeared until what was left was one man and one horse that co-existed—each stronger for what they had given up.

George felt Dusty's muscles relax and his head lower and he knew that something major had taken place in the stallion's mind. He stopped the horse and looked up at the sky and thanked God for helping him feel alive again. He jumped down and loosened the cinch, then walked to the front of the horse and rubbed its head. The horse took a deep breath and George pulled out the other carrot from his pocket and offered it as a peace offering to the Mustang. When he finally pulled off the saddle to walk back to the barn, the Mustang followed him closely. George collapsed in the hay and fell asleep.

When Violet woke up and saw George gone from the corral and the Mustang still sweaty, she knew he had fallen asleep in the barn. She felt different this morning. Freer. She decided not to think about her loss today, but to think about her and George and their future. She walked out and playfully kicked George in the leg. "Wake up!" she said teasingly. Grandpa sat up, surprised, as Grandma sat next to him in the hay. "Let's talk," she said, as she grabbed his hand and held it tight and let the new words flow.

A year later my mother was born. Unlike her brother Donald, she was a fighter. Although she was born with spina bifida, the little baby girl fought her way through life as hard as Grandpa fought the mustang stallion that night and Grandma poured all of the love for both babies into one. My mother, and her two sisters and brother, grew up riding the Mustang, when she didn't have casts on her legs from the surgeries. They buried Dusty when he was twenty-three years old, near the grave of baby Don on the old homestead in Idaho.

Cheryl Dudley

The Quiet Man

My treasures do not clink, they gleam in the sunlight and neigh in the night.

Ancient Bedouin saying

Okay, I'll admit it; my wife, Crystal, fell deeply in love with me quicker than I fell for her. I guess that's why it came as a shock when I found out after we were engaged that there was another man in her life. Long before horses filled our lives, he was there. I began to hear stories of a tall, slim handsome fellow who would meet her at work and take her to lunch. Sure, she was still in love with me, but there was a piece of her committed to someone else, a special someone. I finally was able to connect the dots and solve the mystery of the identity of the man I could never displace. A man, not my competition, but the standard by which I would have to measure up—her father.

James (Jimmy) E. Morris was a quiet man, a strong spiritual man with a peaceful presence about him. Nicknamed "Slats" for his toothpick-style legs, he had a calming influence with everyone he encountered. Slats seemed to always know which way to go, what to think, do, or where to be, in order to be safe and on course. A WWII veteran of the Army

Air Corp, Slats flew bombers over Europe. His priorities of God, family and country were ever present and Jimmy's unconditional love for his daughter always evident.

Years later in our marriage, as we were making plans to establish our simple horse farm, Jimmy was diagnosed with Alzheimer's. Jimmy and Mary, Crystal's mother, moved in with us and we relocated to the city where Jimmy could receive better care. Over the next couple of years, the disease stole away precious moments of now, but never the memories of times gone by. Crystal and her father talked and laughed about events from long ago as if they happened yesterday. She watched her father grow increasingly distant and unresponsive, the quiet man being silenced by a ravaging disease.

Meanwhile, a calm and gentle character with a huge heart had been born, although it would be a while before he and Crystal would cross paths. With four spindly legs of his own and a head too big, no one imagined he would ever grow into a thing of beauty. Then one day when he was nearly two years old, Crystal was visiting the farm where he lived. He came to the fence line where she was walking and followed every step she made until he captured her attention, then her heart. She wasn't looking for a companion, but God knew she needed one, a special one and he was it. She called me right there on the spot about "her find." She has said, time and again, that she can't describe what happened at that moment but the encounter changed her forever.

"Slats" would have also been a wonderful nickname for this tall, slim, handsome fellow whose skinny legs were too long and knobby, but he was called Sundance instead. As it turns out, it is a more descriptive and fitting name for this wonderful Spotted Saddle Horse. He is the warmth of sunshine, chasing away the cold feelings of darkness just like light. This was truly the right name for him. His one blue eye seemed to be a special window allowing us to look deep into his soul and see pure, unconditional love looking back.

Over the next few months, Sundance grew—not just

stronger, but seemingly taller and taller and taller. He was filling out to have incredible strength, as if he knew there was a heavy burden waiting. Crystal would spend hours grooming, training and talking—doing all the wonderful things that build a bond between a woman and her horse nearly as strong as between a mother and her child. And Sundance seemed to know his mission was to nurture and protect Crystal's heart, soul and spirit.

During the next few years, Sundance seemed to complement the role Crystal's dad could no longer fulfill only in the manner of a great trail horse. Each day he assumed a bigger part in helping Crystal to feel complete. The void that was growing by the advancing disease and the heartache it left was quickly being filled with love and affection from Sundance. The same way Jimmy guided Crystal on life's trail, Sundance became a guide on the trails where a fulfilling life can be found. Crystal and Sundance shared miles and miles of riding, absorbing nature's healing beauty, perfection and peace.

It is nearly impossible to describe the life of a caregiver and the toll the duty takes on the soul. Crystal never balked or thought twice about this chance she had to return so much love to her parents. Sundance also never balked at refilling her supply to give. The stress, fatigue and sadness that would envelop Crystal through the long hours of caring for her dad and supporting her mother emotionally would dissolve within a few minutes of being in the saddle. I welcomed the sight of her getting ready for a trail ride escape, knowing the person who came home at the end of the ride would be recharged spiritually and emotionally. Like Jimmy, Sundance was ever watchful for Crystal's safety, never failing to know where to go, what to do and always willing to try.

We miss Jimmy's physical presence now, but I feel his wonderful calming spirit in the new "quiet man" in Crystal's life. Just as Jimmy gave of himself to others, Sundance does the same. He stands in order for blind children to "see" what a horse "looks like" by their touch. He is the first riding experience for people, young and old, who are normally too scared to try, but his peacefulness reaches out and draws them in. His eagerness to go, to fly in his gait, to stay on course wherever they may be heading, is remarkable for even the most experienced horse lover. There is no price to be placed on his ability and devoted companionship.

I watch as he works magic in Crystal's heart. When Crystal is down, he comes down too—down to pick her spirit up. He grazes nearby, keeping watch over her while she sits among the flowers thinking, praying or hoping. Crystal thinks she is watching over him, but I know the real truth. When Crystal is happy, Sundance exudes excitement. He'll jump in the trailer ready for new adventures, to swim rivers, climb hills and confidently tackle any challenge ahead.

I am forever grateful for what this wonderful horse has done for my wife. Crystal's relationship with him is as strong as any could be between a horse and their human companion. I know she loves me more than life itself, but I welcome this other fellow and all the love she has for him into our lives. I praise this new quiet man who came along at a time to rescue the spirit of such a wonderful woman. He has taken care of her in ways only one of God's most marvelous creatures can. This tri-colored beauty with one crystal blue eye has given himself in ways that would make her original quiet man, oh, so proud and grateful.

Tom Maupin

Let Me Say "Thank You"

Find a purpose in life so big it will challenge every capacity to be at your best.

David O. McKay

I remember the first time I got on a horse. I was two years old and we were watching a friend of the family ride. My mom agreed to let me take a short ride around the arena with the friend and that was it! I was horse crazy. From then on, I drove my parents insane begging for a horse. Whenever I saw a horse, I would beg even harder.

When I was four years old, my life as I know it now began. I have Selective Mutism. This is a rare childhood disorder in which children stop speaking in certain social situations, many times at around the age of four. I spoke normally to my parents, my brother and certain other people, but was silent at school and in social situations. I went days, weeks, months without a sound at school. At most, I might quietly whisper to a friend.

Often, children with Selective Mutism will not speak in the presence of others; even to a person they normally talk to. There is a lot of whispering in ears, so that others cannot hear. We have normal or above average IQs and usually no speech pathology. The most important factor in this disorder is, we cannot speak. We do not do this purposely or willfully, it feels impossible to speak. As you can imagine, many children are blamed, punished and traumatized, especially at school. The disorder is believed to be anxiety related and treatment is difficult, but not impossible. We have so much more to learn.

My parents searched for a cure. At that time, we did not even have a name for what I had. I suffered silently through school until I was ten years old when one in a long string of psychologists had an idea. Having discussed his plan with my parents beforehand, one day in my therapy session I was asked by the psychologist what I wanted more than anything in the world. He explained that I was going to be given an opportunity to work for what I wanted. I couldn't believe my good luck, but I could not answer. I just stood there struggling to verbalize what I wanted more than anything else in the world. Finally, I was permitted to whisper the answer in my mother's ear. "A horse," was all I could say.

I was to get a pony, but before we could even start looking, I had to live up to my end of the bargain. I had to try to talk. I had a chart of weekly tasks I had to accomplish. I had to answer the phone five times per week, something I had never done before. I had to make five phone calls to my friends. I had to say one word to my teacher at school and the list went on. For a child with Selective Mutism, saying one word to someone can be like climbing Mount Everest.

I did everything that was asked of me and the day came when my parents found a local riding stable that had the perfect pony. His name was Sequoia, a strong little chestnut with some roaning and a tiny white spot on his rump. He was perfect, of course, and I fell in love immediately. We boarded him at the riding stable and I began taking lessons. I wanted to be the best I could be and I swelled with pride every time I got on Sequoia. It truly was a dream come true. I learned to brush him, saddle him, pick his hooves out. Each week I could not wait for Saturday and my lesson, then my free time with my Sequoia. When I was in Sequoia's presence, I forgot all about my problems and felt strong and secure.

As I see it, horses are silent too, but they are fast, powerful and free at the same time. Horses give me the strength I lack. They give me a reason to push myself, when I can find no other. Horses have been part of my life for well over twenty years now, all the while helping me deal with an isolating, frightening disorder. When things get difficult, as they still sometimes do, I go to my horses. With them, I can be silent, but I can hold my head up and have dignity and freedom. By connecting with them, I have learned to embrace what I was once shunned for and I found my voice.

I am a fully participating member of society these days. My horses and I made it through a master's degree and then law school. I am a practicing attorney, I even make court appearances. I may have made it otherwise, but I'm not sure. I feel I owe my life to the horse and I try to give it back to them every day. I am fortunate that I can look out my back door and see my beautiful horses looking back at me. I am so grateful that I get to watch them run in their mountain pasture every day. I hope I never stop learning from them. They have given me the best gift I could ever imagine, my life.

Kim Morton

The Little Horse That Heals

Better to light one small candle than to curse the darkness.

Chinese Proverb

We had just finished unwrapping Christmas gifts on the morning of December 20, 1999, and were ready for our traditional holiday breakfast when I said, "Wait, there is one more gift to see!" December 25th was not only a religious holiday, a world-wide celebration, Santa's big day. It was also my dad Robert's birthday. I had gotten up early this morning and secretly headed over to the stable. Hidden on the side of my residential home were my truck and horse trailer. No one knew what was to come.

With my family assembled in anticipation of another surprise, I carefully led my father's eighty-fourth birthday present into the family room. Red-felt reindeer antlers adorned his head, he sported a handsome green halter and a winter's growth of hair seemed to add fifty pounds to his 31" tall frame. A stunned silence quickly gave way to squeals of delight and laughter. There wasn't a dry eye in the house as I handed the lead line to my father and said, "Happy birthday, Dad!" During the past year, Dad had casually mentioned, "Gee, I would sure like to have one of those miniature horses." This was a significant change . . . this was doable—the last horse he coveted was a Clydesdale!

His name was Rebel, a moniker certainly bestowed as a joke since his personality and temperament would prove to be anything but. I found Rebel just three days before from an ad in the paper. A kind description of the conditions in which I found him would be a puppy mill. When the owner brought Rebel out for me to see, he literally had a live monkey hanging from his neck and a dead-eyed look of unhappiness and toleration. He was completely uncared for. I took him immediately.

I brought Rebel to the stable of a therapeutic riding program for people with special needs where I am a certified riding instructor. At Horses Help, I got Rebel settled in, had our vet check him over and groomed him until the day of his big debut arrived. It was immediately clear that Rebel had the perfect disposition to be a certified therapy horse. There were bigger things in store for this little guy than being the perfect birthday gift.

Soon it became necessary for Rebel to have a real job and we taught him how to pull a cart. At first, the idea of actually working instead of just eating and looking cute didn't sit well with Rebel, but he eventually took to it easily and joined an eight horse and cart drill team. He now performs all over Arizona at horse shows and fairs in a fifteen-minute program filled with resounding, patriotic music. At Horses Help, Rebel lives among fourteen big horses of all sizes and shapes, and we use him to help children get used to the larger animals by leading and grooming him. Dad comes every Tuesday to visit, delighted to own a horse but have none of the responsibilities of its care.

One of my interests lies in animal-assisted therapy and the elderly, so it wasn't long before Rebel and I became the only miniature horse Delta Pet Partner therapy team in the entire state of Arizona. In two years, we have visited over twenty care centers for the elderly. Rebel's expertise turns out to be patients afflicted with Alzheimer's or dementia. Instinctively, he seems to know that he must spend more time, to wait for a reaction, when he encounters a person with cognitive impairment. Time and time again, he quietly rests his head on a bed or a wheelchair, waiting patiently for a hand to be raised or a voice to be heard, but with someone else, he might allow a quick pat and move on. On one visit to a day-care facility for the elderly, he quickly made his way through the crowd of almost eighty residents. My heart swelled with pride when he hesitated longer with two women, sitting at opposite ends of the room, that were blind and needed more time to "see" with their hands. On another occasion, we visited a woman who was about to die and Rebel gently laid his head near her hand so she could pet him. He somehow knew she needed him in her last few hours of life. We can't teach this, it is simply in a creature's heart. It is a gift and every time I watch my little horse bring a smile to a face or a tear to the eye, I am blessed with the most incredible feeling of joy and pride and fulfillment.

No one told Rebel he isn't the size of a draft horse. If they had, he wouldn't have believed them anyway. He doesn't know he was born premature, abandoned by his mother and, at one point in his life, wasn't very well cared for. From the start, this scrappy little guy just followed his heart as he chased the big horses in the pastures. Rebel still follows his heart as he faithfully clip-clops up the steps, in the elevators and down the halls of hospitals, schools and nursing homes, past noisy respirators to visit his special people. He doesn't know that horses don't usually do that, either.

Rebel doesn't see the Alzheimer's, the hospital beds, the blindness, the wheelchairs, or the fear in the eyes of those who feel unsafe, just like he doesn't see size. But he does see the smiles and the joy. Even dressed up in bright red reindeer antlers, he quietly demonstrates what he's known all along; life is good, people are good. If Rebel could talk, he would probably ask, "What size is positive attitude? How tall is success? How big is love?" This funny little horse doesn't know or even care. He simply goes about his business in a great big way, gently showing every one he touches that none of us is small and everyone counts.

Another Christmas day found Rebel and me at a care center for the elderly that we frequent. I had Rebel loaded up on the trailer, ready to go when down the sidewalk came a woman frantically pushing her husband in a wheelchair. "Did I miss him? Oh dear, did I miss him?" Her face beheld desperation, disappointment and sadness, even panic. I will never forget that look. Sitting in the wheelchair was a tall man, seemingly unaware of his surroundings, his head cocked to one side and an empty look on his face.

"I was just about to leave. Do you think your husband would like to meet Rebel?" I asked.

"I just don't know anymore," she answered, with so much sadness and loss of hope that my heart broke.

"Let me get Rebel out. Let's try."

I led Rebel over to this shell of a man. As usual, Rebel put his head on the man's lap and just waited. Sure enough, up came a hand, reaching weakly for Rebel's muzzle. Then, the man's head rose and a slight moan escaped from his lips, "Rebel." His wife was in awe. It had been a very long time since her husband had responded to anything or anyone. I could visibly see her despair soften as Rebel continued to visit with her husband.

"Thank you," she said softly, gently stroking her husband's shoulder, "you and Rebel have given me the best Christmas present ever."

Leslie A. Paradise with Jan Clare

Helping Hooves

*When walking through the "valley of shad-
ows," remember, a shadow is cast by a light.*

H.K. Barclay

Watching Auggie ride the big gelding around the ring, his
mother is amazed at how far he has come. While other children his age play T-ball or little league soccer, Auggie struggles with everyday tasks like walking down the hall or
building a tower with toy blocks. His parents rejoice in small
accomplishments—the first time he caught a ball and each
new word he learns.

When Auggie was ten months old, his doctors diagnosed
him with delayed development. Children with delayed development fail to reach developmental milestones at an appro-
priate age. For example, Auggie did not begin walking at the
same age as other children and he still has trouble talking.

Auggie's parents learned about the HELP Center in
Austin, Texas—a facility offering therapeutic riding lessons
to children. The goal of HELP is to focus on the rider's abilities, not his disabilities. By working with parents and other
professionals, the center provides exercise and motivation to
their riders.

When he began riding at the age of two, Auggie could not sit upright on his horse. He frequently tipped forward until his helmet rested on his horse's neck. Volunteers walked on either side of his horse to keep Auggie in the saddle. He also did not communicate with the volunteers verbally and he got frustrated whenever anyone misunderstood his attempts at communication.

Auggie met Trio at the HELP Center and she was a turning point for him. Linda runs the center where she teaches lessons, feeds the horses and recruits volunteers. She also volunteers with a rescue group, and she found Trio while attending an auction on behalf of the rescue. When Linda first saw Trio, the horse was standing in the corner of the crowded pen. She tried to stay out of the way of the bigger horses but they continually bumped into her as they jostled to get to the small pile of hay on the ground. Trio's light gray coat was hidden by a layer of caked mud. But beneath the shaggy hair, layers of grime and dull coat, Linda saw a beautiful equine soul. When Trio fixed her dark brown eyes on her, Linda knew this mare needed a special home. The auction began and before long Trio was ushered into the ring. The auctioneer began his chant, but no one wanted the dingy pony. Finally, a rescue volunteer raised her hand. The auctioneer shouted, *"SOLD!"* and Linda was soon loading Trio into a trailer for the short trip to her new home.

The volunteers at the center fell in love with Trio. They spent hours grooming, petting and bathing her. They fattened her up by feeding her several meals a day. Within weeks, she was transformed into a sleek, gorgeous gray pony who basked in the attention of the volunteers and children at the HELP Center.

Trio's laid-back personality was perfect, and the staff began testing her suitability for therapy work. They led her through a busy arena where kids were chatting, laughing, crying and even screaming, and Trio carefully followed her leader. Volunteers threw balls over her back and rolled them under her belly. Trio watched the balls but never moved a

step. Children tossed balls and plastic rings at Trio's sides;
again, she only watched the children and never even
flinched. Trio readily walked up to the mounting block and
wheelchair ramp. She negotiated between jump standards
and around buckets without taking a wrong step.
Volunteers rode her in lessons and she was perfect, stopping
when she heard the word "whoa" and keeping her body
underneath her rider when the rider was off-balance. She
played games like ring-toss and basketball from horseback.
Trio was ready to begin therapy work.

Finally, the big day came. As a volunteer groomed and
tacked Trio up, Linda spoke to the little gray pony. "Trio
today is a big day. You begin helping very special kids. Your
first rider is a boy named Auggie. When he first came here he
couldn't talk to us and couldn't sit upright on his horse.
Now he says a few words, laughs and sits up straight when
he rides. Take care of Auggie, Trio. This is your new job."
Linda helped Auggie onto Trio and they began the lesson.
Auggie and Trio walked around the arena and weaved
through buckets with the help of volunteers. Auggie tossed
rings into buckets and sat on Trio backwards to throw a basketball into a hoop. During his lesson, one of the riders next
door was practicing his jumping. Auggie stopped throwing
the ball to watch the jumper and then pointed at the jumper.

"Do you want to ride like that, Auggie?" Linda asked.
"Yeah!" was the emphatic reply.

Although the kids at the center do not have the motor
skills to ride a jumper, they have their own "jump" that con-
sists of two jump standards with a ground pole. However, to
jump the rider must be able to give verbal commands, main-
tain a modified jump position and stop and steer the horse
on his own. Auggie's instructor thought his impaired motor
and verbal skills would keep him from being able to jump
with Trio.

Auggie's instructor explained this to him and he watched
her intently. As soon as she was done, Auggie, who had
been quiet during his lesson, sat up straighter and told Trio,

"Walk on!" in a loud voice. Auggie's instructor decided to let him steer Trio, and Auggie amazed his mother and the staff when he flawlessly maneuvered Trio through the gate into a small arena that contained a few jumps. He told Trio, "Whoa," and pulled the reins back to his belly—a move he had never made before.

Auggie's accomplishments for the day were only just beginning. Still doubtful that Auggie could manage to stay in the modified jump position used by the riders at HELP, his instructor helped him lean forward over Trio's neck, curl his fingers around the blanket for balance and keep his back straight. The instructor reminded Auggie to look through Trio's ears instead of down at her neck.

Auggie told Trio, "Walk on. One, two, three, trot. Jump please!" This was quite a mouthful for him, but it came out without a glitch as Trio walked toward the ground pole set up as a jump between two standards. When he came away from the jump, Auggie was grinning from ear to ear!

In the past few years, Auggie's motor skills, communication and confidence have all improved. That first day he jumped Trio showed everyone exactly how far he had come. Auggie continues to improve, now running around the HELP Center, petting the horses and frequently jumping during his lesson.

While Trio helped Auggie, Auggie also helped Trio. Because of her training at the HELP Center, Trio found a home with children who love her—she'll never again be a dirty, unwanted, unloved pony.

Jennifer Williams, Ph.D.

A Gambler's Instinct

To consider constantly the comfort and happiness of another is not a sign of weakness but of strength.

Charles Conrad

A mutual love of horses created an inseparable bond between my father and me. We spent countless hours preparing for horse shows and riding the quiet trails near our house. Horses brought joy into our family, whether it was from a ribbon at the fair or participating in the local apple orchard's annual fall "train robbery," where we would race up to the train on horseback and demand fresh-picked apples as ransom. Our horses soon became more like family than pets. Mixed in with the good times were periods of grief and sorrow.

As any horse lover knows, an affectionate nuzzle or a good morning nicker brings happiness and soothes the soul during dark times. This is never more true than when debilitating disease brings pain and suffering to the patient and his or her family. My father's two-year battle with cancer gave our family a firsthand account of the pain and suffering caused by disease. Throughout his treatments, he could not help but notice the number of young children being treated for cancer and during a three-week stay in an intensive care unit, he made a vow that once he was well again, he would try and bring a bit of happiness to these children's lives. My father returned home from the hospital more determined than ever to share the joy of horses with children fighting their own battles with cancer.

In the spring, the perfect opportunity presented itself: a family-oriented picnic sponsored by a local community out-reach group whose mission was to provide support for children with cancer and their families. Children's laughter filled the air and sunshine warmed everyone's mood. My father and I arrived early in the morning with two horses, both five-year-old Quarter Horses, new to the family, but up to the task of giving these youngsters a few moments of freedom and enjoyment. Chip and Gambler had not been on our farm long and could be on the frisky side at times, but both seemed to sense the fragility of their young riders, rose to the occasion and were the perfect mounts.

By the end of the day, a crisp fall breeze was settling and both horses were tired from the day's activities, having carried between twenty and thirty riders each. As we readied them for the trip home, my father noticed a young boy in a wheelchair off to the side arguing with his parents. Dad had spotted him earlier in the day, but noticed the distance his parents kept between the horses and the child. Quietly, he approached the boy and his parents and reassured them that Gambler, although tall at 16.1-hands, was nothing more than a teddy bear with four long legs that would be gentle with their son.

Tears filled their eyes as they expressed appreciation, but began to explain it was not a fear of the horse but the physical condition of their son that forced them to admire the horses from afar. Gingerly, they pulled back the boy's blanket to reveal an endless maze of tubes feeding him medication. My father asked them to wait a moment as he rushed over and grabbed Gambler's reins from my hands. With a soft voice, he led Gambler to the boy's wheelchair. As he approached, he explained to the little boy that the horse's name was Gambler, that he really liked children and how Gambler loved pats on the nose. As if Gambler could sense the gravity of the situation, he very carefully dropped his whole head into the boy's lap and gently let out a contended sigh while the youngster stroked his white blaze.

A smile stretched from ear-to-ear as the boy kissed Gambler good-bye and said thank you. Gambler's instinctive nuzzle of the young boy soothed the souls of many onlookers who witnessed the exchange that afternoon.

Although we never saw that little boy again, we know that for a brief moment that day he forgot about the invasive tubes and the constant pain from his disease. The memory of his smile is an ongoing source of hope and inspiration for my father who has continued to use his love of horses to benefit children with cancer.

Kathryn Navarra

Peanut

We meet to create memories and part to cherish them.

Indian proverb

"Mother! Would you please get rid of this pony! He doesn't do anything anymore. He's useless. And senile!"

Just like great-uncle Trevor came instantly into my mind.

My son was grumbling unkindly as he dragged our ancient, small pony, Peanut, past the kitchen window. He'd been sent to retrieve the elder equine after a neighbor had called, again, to say Peanut was sleeping on her back porch.

Okay. So my son was right. Peanut had outlived his usefulness, just like great-uncle Trevor. The children had long since erased the memory of riding him, forgetting how much easier his size made their bravery the first time I unsnapped the longe line and they were on their own. They no longer dressed him up as a troll on Halloween or hitched him to their Flexible Flyer when it snowed.

Like the eccentric relative everyone wished would stay in the attic, Peanut had become an embarrassment, a crow in a barn full of peacocks. He was low in productivity and high in maintenance, as so often the elderly become. His tiny feet grew alarmingly fast and needed frequent and pricey visits from our blacksmith. The pony's skin occasionally developed strange rashes requiring exotic cream and special order brushes. One eye was cloudy and he had a noticeable limp.

He had to be turned out in a far pasture alone because he was so annoying to the other horses. Peanut had to be *right* next to whatever horse was in his pasture. Any horse turned out with the little pony, even one with the kindest disposition, was soon vexed enough to aim a kick at the nuisance next to them, most of the time landing way above the pony. But the limp resulted from a kick that connected.

During Peanut's annual checkup, the vet assured us that, even with his problems, the pony was in very good shape for his age and the limp, while permanent, wasn't painful. In other words, there was no real reason to put him down; inconvenience doesn't count.

He reminded me of our great-uncle Trevor, my grandfather's eldest brother, because I recall our large family feeling much the same way about him. Like Peanut, great-uncle Trevor often wandered off and forgot his way home. He'd appear at family gatherings and do or say something so outrageous everyone would talk about it for months.

When I was six, I thought him wonderful company. We'd often take walks together and he'd let me talk and talk about all the things I loved but didn't interest the rest of my family. It hurt my feelings when an aunt or uncle would whisper, "I wish Trevor would just stay out of the way."

Fortunately, with the luck of the Irish in his favor, a funny little old widow who thought him quite marvelous discovered great-uncle Trevor. She had a comfortable pension and developed a grand passion for the man everyone wanted somewhere else. They married when he was eighty-one and she turned seventy-nine, living quite happily for many more years, even though the rest of the family forever referred to them as the "dotty duo."

But Peanut wasn't a person. He was simply a silly, undersized, old pony that escaped often from his pasture, needed his hay watered down, his food pulverized and daily medicine for his conditions and who annoyed all the other horses and most of the family. Maybe it was time to think about a send-off to the big pasture in the sky, I pondered, watching the teensy equine shuffle after my irritated son. Instead, I divided a paddock and put chicken wire between the rails to keep Peanut from escaping through them. I double-bolted the gate when he learned how to slip the latch. Is he really worth all the trouble? After all, I was the only one who paid any attention to him at all.

Until one day late in March.

It was a spring teaser, the first morning that dawned without snow on the ground. I was brushing the dogs on the porch when I noticed a figure at the far end of the lane where Peanut's paddock ended. Peering more closely I saw a tall man with a black overcoat, his wispy gray hair blowing in the lovely breeze. He carried a cane in one hand and something orange in the other. Peanut was standing with his nose as high as he could put it over the fence, piqued by whatever the elderly gentleman was holding.

I walked to the end of the lane and the man turned slowly and smiled, introducing himself as Matthew, the father-in-law of a friend of mine who lived two farms over the hill. Due to several infirmities of old age, Matthew had recently moved in with his daughter and was taking a stroll to get to know the neighborhood.

"This is a very, very, fine pony," Matthew said, offering more from a full bunch of carrots he carried.

"Long ago I rode," he smiled in remembrance, "and I recall there was nothing as fine as talking to my horse. I didn't ride well, but I loved wandering the countryside at a walk. I wonder," he added, "would you mind terribly if I visited this fine pony on my walks? It seems he likes to talk to me, too and that's so very pleasing to the soul."

I assured Matthew I'd be delighted to have him converse with Peanut. "My children have outgrown him and I think he'd love to feel useful again," I said.

"Yes," replied Matthew, softly, "I think I know about that."

As the weeks passed, the conversation between Matthew and Peanut expanded when one day the old gentleman asked if he could put a "leash" on Peanut and take him along on his strolls.

The pony was happier than I had seen him in years. Each day I could see him standing at the very end of his paddock peering through the chicken wire as he waited for his friend to come and walk him. And Matthew never missed a day. Soon the "leash" was unnecessary and I watched Peanut and Matthew slowly saunter side-by-side, up and down the dusty road, both limping slightly, the pony munching carrots and Matthew puffing on his pipe. They'd frequently stop and share conversation with other acquaintances along the way, but clearly their most important discussions were between the two of them.

Watching them I reminded the children that, human or equine, one could be quite useful in many ways for a very long time. And each day I thanked the powers that be that Peanut had found a friend who realized, appearances and oddities aside, just how wonderful he really was.

The day Matthew didn't show up, I knew the worst had happened and I was right. My friend called that morning to tell me the old gentleman had passed away in his sleep. Peanut kept vigil by the fence for three days. Then he simply lay down and never got up again.

If there's a heaven and I'm certain there is, I believe Matthew and Peanut are taking celestial strolls, deep in conversation with each other . . . and maybe great-uncle Trevor.

Cooky McClung

Not All Art Hangs in Galleries

God forbid I should go to any heaven where there are no horses.

R.B. Cunningham Graham

"So, tell me about your new horse," my mother asked.

What I had called my mom about was her surgery the next day and to finalize our plans for my coming over to help her when she came home from the hospital in two days. I hadn't even planned on mentioning the new horse. My mom was a city kid who always loved animals, horses included, but had never learned how to ride. But she always supported my love of horses and so I told her about my as yet unnamed rescue horse. I told her how a friend had this little mare, an underfed palomino Paint, dumped on him and that she was very gentle. I hoped to be able to train her for my children to ride.

I still remember that conversation. I was talking on the portable phone while standing out on my back porch, watching the little golden mare down in the pasture. It was the last time I ever talked with my mother.

The next day, I was in town buying shoes when a great fear suddenly washed over me. I thought of my mom's surgery, stopped in mid-purchase and rushed home to call the hospital. It took a while to get information but something was going wrong. She had been in recovery but they had rushed her back into surgery. Many frantic phone calls later, information trickled back to me. Bleeding in her brain, doctors trying to stop the bleeding, ICU, intercranial pressure, the news was all terrible. Absolutely terrible.

I rushed over to the town where she lived, a three-hour drive. It was hot summertime and she was unconscious in the ICU as the whole family descended in a panic. Tempers flared like the heat. None of us were prepared for this.

The weeks that followed were hell. Mom's intercranial pressure came back down and the doctors were able to wean her off the respirator. They got her out of ICU and into a regular hospital bed. But she remained in a coma, unconscious and unresponsive. Brain damage had occurred and we waited to see what and how much.

Through those weeks, I was in a dream state. I drove back and forth between my town and hers every several days, where I would sit beside her in the hospital and sing to her for hours, hoping against hope that my voice would reach into her private prison and comfort her. Then back home again, driving across the desert in my rickety truck with no air conditioning, back to my farm and children to take care of my responsibilities there. And to replenish my spirit.

Out in the pasture, my new horse grazed, my little golden mare. I had no time to even halter her, although occasionally I would walk out to check her and to lean on her shoulder and breathe her sweet horse scent. But mostly, I watched her from my back porch, a ray of sunshine out in my green pasture, the only spot of light, it seemed, in my increasingly desperate world.

Every time I traveled to see my mom, she looked worse. The longer she went without recovering consciousness, the worse the prognosis. The doctors did brain scans, told me the grim news and we moved her to a hospice. I got done what needed to be done. My mother was my best friend, my cheerleader, my mentor and the one person who believed in me when no one else did. And she was slowly dying before my eyes and there was nothing I could do to help her. Outside, I was numb, just going through the motions. Inside, I was clinging to the vision of the little golden mare, glowing in the sunshine down in the green pastures.

My mother died five weeks after a surgery she thought would improve her life. She had been looking forward to regaining her ability to drive a car and not being dependent. Instead, she had a surgical accident and never awoke. I consoled myself that at least she never had to wake to the realization of what had happened to her; she never had to lose her hope. There was only one way left for her to achieve independence and that was to walk the pathway to the spirit world. There is not a day that goes by that I don't miss her.

What got me through those terrible days were the kindness of friends and a vision of beauty, a splash of golden sunlight in a terribly dark world. For those of us who truly love horses, we don't have to ride them, even touch them, for them to bring us great joy and comfort. The value of a horse goes beyond its use. Its utility is in simply being what it is. Sometimes just seeing a horse calmly grazing in a green pasture is all we need.

People pay great amounts of money for works of art that hang on their walls. It is not alive, but comes alive inside them when it touches their hearts with wonder. But not all art hangs in galleries. Sometimes it walks in our fields like golden sunlight.

Janice Willard, D.V.M., M.S.

The Winged Horse

Being defeated is often only a temporary condition. Giving up is what makes it permanent.

Marilyn vos Savant

When Wendy was really tiny, her grandfather used to tell her many stories. Being a man of some learning, he used to tell her tales based on Greek mythology and it didn't take her long to have a favorite. "Tell me the stories about Pegasus, the Winged Horse" was her constant plea.

The little cottage where Wendy and her family lived was on the land owned by the local estate. The field beside their cottage was home to about four horses and they were the love of Wendy's life. She talked to them, got picked up to feed and pat them and they soon got to know her. One of them in particular, Lucky Eric, would come trotting over as soon as he heard her young, high voice call out to him.

It was Wendy's dream to learn to ride a pony and then a horse, and her parents were meticulously putting a little money away every month to try and get her into the local riding school.

Unfortunately, it was about this time that she began to feel unwell. She was sick and then totally lethargic. After many weeks of tests, she was diagnosed with a rare bone disease and many, many months of painful treatment followed for her.

Once her condition was stabilized, her parents were told that Wendy's legs would always be very weak and she would have trouble balancing. As soon as she could, Wendy, now very frail, was back out at the fence calling to the horses. Just as if she had never been away, Lucky Eric came bounding over and as her father lifted her up, he rubbed his face against hers and then gave a loud snort. Wendy giggled, laughed and told her father that the horse had told her that he missed her.

They spoke to her doctor and he was adamant that Wendy would never be able to ride a horse. They were heartbroken, but fortunately, the owner of the estate heard about how ill Wendy had been. His wife, Alicia, called on them to see how she was progressing and learned of the problems. She was there when Wendy went out in her father's arms to see "her" horses.

A week later Alicia arrived in her riding gear and with a kind of harness. "I have come to take Wendy riding!" she announced.

She explained that she would take Wendy on the horse with her, strap the harness round them both to keep her upright and they would ride together. It all sounded very risky to Wendy's mum, but she knew how much this could mean to her brave daughter.

Out they went and when Wendy asked which horse and was told, "Lucky Eric, of course. He is just dying to take you out for a ride," there was no turning back!

That first day they just went for a little jog, but as it all seemed to work well and it gave Wendy such happiness, they went a little further each time they went out.

One day with the sun shining and a strong breeze blowing, Alicia gave Lucky Eric his head. She felt sometimes that this beautiful and sensitive horse knew exactly the fragility of the little package he was carrying. Every time she took

Wendy with her, he talked more and he responded to the slightest instruction, so this day she gave him more freedom. They went a little faster and Wendy giggled in delight. Seeing the small hedge in front of them, Alicia urged Lucky Eric on and he sailed over it as Wendy screamed in pleasure.

That night she couldn't wait to tell her granddad, "I flew, Granddad. Lucky Eric was just like Pegasus, we just flew through the air, it was wonderful!"

Alicia had to explain to them that they had barely left the ground and they should not worry that she had been rash with her precious charge. It was as Wendy went off for another ride that her grandfather looked at her parents. "All things are relative, when you can barely walk and when you are up on top of the thing you love most in life, one foot off the ground is flying!"

As Wendy grew up, she underwent a new treatment that helped her enormously. Her parents knew she would never be robust, but she could walk unaided and she learned to ride, Alicia saw to that. When she was twenty-one, she had a good job and she had her own horse. At her twenty-first birthday party, amidst all the presents and the fun, her mother found her staring out of the kitchen window toward the field where Lucky Eric used to come running to see her.

Wendy had tears running down her face as she turned. "I was thinking back to those days when I was so ill and to all the wonderful times I had with Lucky Eric. You know, Mum, being told that I would be able to walk unaided came second to those days I went flying on Lucky Eric; he really was my winged horse!"

Joyce Stark

The Glory of an Imperfect Resurrection

*For man there are only three important events:
birth, life and death; but he is unaware of being
born, he suffers when he dies and he forgets to live.*

Jean De La Bruyere

Easter of 1995 had nothing to do with resurrection or life.
The Saturday before Easter, I was diagnosed with aggressive,
stage-four non-Hodgkin's lymphoma. The only good news
was that I didn't have any cancer cells in my spinal fluid, indi-
cating that the cancer had not spread to my brain. Every other
major organ was affected.

Someone else would have thought about their children, but
I had no children. Others would have thought about their
spouse, but I had no husband. I thought about my nephew,
Patrick, who was not yet five, but he had a mother who
already loved him beyond all measure. I thought about my
mother and realized the news would devastate her, but she
had other children, including Patrick's mother who lived on
the same property. By human standards, I believed myself
fairly expendable.

My greatest sorrow that day in the intensive care unit at
Cleveland University Hospital did not include my own life. I

had been in and out of intensive care and in one hospital or another for the last five months. I was so weak I could not change position in bed. My hair had been falling out for weeks from massive doses of prednisone. I needed a machine to push air into my lungs past the tumors in my bronchi. I had pretty much decided that a loving God would have ended my life months before as a kindness.

No. I only thought about a promise I had made to a strong-willed bay filly that was coming three that April. I had promised her that she would never be broken like so many horses. By breeding, Mandy was a National Show Horse, three-quarters Arabian and one-quarter American Saddlebred. In reality, she was a trash filly destined for the slaughter sale in Sugarcreek, Ohio, because she was born the wrong color. I paid $200 (meat price) for the neglected filly and she had grown to be my dream horse—beautiful and intelligent and totally oblivious to the violence that so many people called training. My death would mean a fate far worse than death for Mandy.

Mandy was counting on me. So, I embarked on a two-year odyssey of high-dose chemotherapy, radiation, bone biopsies, spinal taps, CT scans, stem cell harvests and bone marrow transplants, blood transfusions, infections, hearing loss, vomiting, alopecia and pain. All to keep a promise to a horse.

When the psychologist suggested I develop a positive vision for the battle raging within my body, I turned to Mandy for inspiration. She rescued me. I closed my eyes and Mandy charged onto the battlefield of my disease with the rage of a mare defending her newborn foal. She trampled cancer cells that took the form of snakes into shapeless pulp in the grass. When Mandy finished destroying the cancer snakes, she came to me glistening with sweat from her brave task. Taking me onto her back, she swept me away from the carnage and pain to the top of a high hill. Looking back from that great height, the battlefield became a familiar meadow filled with wild flowers. I knew I was home and safe and free of the nightmare below. I smelled the sweet saltiness of a sweaty horse, felt the swell of her ribs beneath me, heard her hooves pound the earth, tasted the wind racing across the grass. For a moment, I blotted out the foul odor of DMSO, a blend of dead fish and rotted garlic used to preserve stem cells for bone marrow transplants.

By the second year, the vision changed. A time came when I could not mount my rescuer. "Let me go," I begged my mom. "Just close the coffin and let me be dead."

"What about Mandy?" she asked quietly. "If I let you go, what will I do with Mandy?"

My mother never quit reminding me of my promise to Mandy. If she minded taking second place to a horse, she never said, and she died without my ever asking.

I could abandon anyone but Mandy, so I wept and closed my eyes tightly and dragged myself into the saddle and clung desperately to her mane for the climb up the hill. I did not look back. The vision was no longer about triumphing over my cancer. It was about simply holding on to Mandy as tightly as I could to survive. I was consumed by depression and looked for some reassurance that my cancer nightmare would end. I needed proof that it was over and decided that riding Mandy for real, not just in my mind, would be that proof.

Somewhere along the line, I also decided that achieving my goal would not count if I asked for help. I would not even ask God for help. After all, it was His fault I would not get to ride Mandy until she was six or more.

I am convinced that God is the Divine Horseman, with a flawless sense of timing and feel, and perfect patience. I turned away in anger time and time again, and he waited for me to find the right answer, no matter how long it took. If I were a horse, I would have been in the remedial round pen.

It took six years for me to ask for help.

It also took shattering my wrist for me to admit I lacked the strength and flexibility, not to mention bone density, to cope with the insecurities of a mature green horse. And I had so successfully protected Mandy from abuse that she regarded most humans with fear that erupted into aggression. When my brother-in-law tried to remove the saddle while my sister took me to the emergency room when I broke my wrist, Mandy attacked him. Eight hours later, as I worked to free Mandy from the saddle under her belly with one hand, I realized I had created a lethal gap in her education. It took six months for my wrist to heal and nearly a year for Mandy to overcome her phobia of a saddle.

As my health improved, my mother's health declined and I cared for her with the same devotion she had given me throughout my illness. Her heart grew weak and our time grew short. Mandy understood and waited for me. Two weeks before Easter 2001, I held my mother's hand as her tired heart stopped. Once again, I found no resurrection for myself among the March daffodils.

Now it was just Mandy and me. Going it alone finally no longer mattered. I turned to the Divine Horseman and asked for help and he opened the gate. He sent me angels—an outspoken friend who granted me no quarter and a horse trainer some called a "horse whisperer" who disliked both titles.

Sherry Lindon introduced me to Clark Howell as "the woman with the problem horse I was telling you about." I was humiliated.

"My horse and I are just a little stuck," I corrected politely, unable to look the tall, raw-boned cowboy in the eye. Mandy's only problem was me.

"Well, . . ." Clark said slowly, "we all get stuck once in a while. The hard part is admitting it."

I knew then that he knew the awful truth. I wondered if he could feel it the same way Mandy did. I had come to the clinic with Sheri to evaluate Clark and decide if I could trust him with Mandy. With one handshake, he knew I no longer trusted myself.

Clark had organized Pat Parelli's first clinic in Ohio and was a long-time apostle of natural horsemanship. He understood Mandy's aggression as the defensiveness of an insecure prey animal. He didn't mind that I took a vacation to hover outside the round pen and watch his every move as he worked Mandy.

Mandy carried a rider successfully on March 9, 2002, nearly six years from the day I was told I had non-Hodgkin's lymphoma. Clark's son, Jesse, had the honor of that first ride and I will always be a little jealous. Ten days later, I rode Mandy myself in Clark's arena.

I never told Clark why I had to have Mandy home for Easter. I could not explain to him how an empty barn could feel like a tomb on Good Friday. Mandy was supposed to be home by Good Friday, but Clark could not deliver her. I'm sure he knew I was standing beside the answering machine, refusing to pick up. No doubt he thought I was angry, but I was crying. The Divine Horseman asked me to wait. Mandy and I both have a problem with waiting for our cues. I was left to contemplate the Saturday before Easter as a holy vigil of memories and broken dreams.

Clark promised to bring Mandy home on Sunday—Easter. I cried a little harder and was very glad I did not pick up the phone. It is too hard to explain such tears. Clark does not know the significance of his words or that yesterday's delays and today's commitments have only made him the instrument of the Divine Horseman. He does not know the redemption and resurrection that is woven into Mandy's homecoming.

Mandy is my Easter present. Like the resurrection of Lazarus, it does not matter if we stumble out of the tomb. The Divine Horseman knows accuracy is more important than speed, that controlling all four corners is the best way to make a turn. It is not necessary to gallop off the battlefield. It is enough to walk away victorious.

I often ride Mandy to the top of the hill that overlooks the meadow in my vision. I smell her sweat, tangle my fingers in her mane and taste the wind that blows between her ears. From her saddle, I am not afraid to look back, or ahead. It is the glory of an imperfect resurrection.

Linda K. Hren

4

A SPECIAL BOND

For want of a nail a shoe was lost, for want of a shoe a horse was lost, for want of a horse a rider was lost, for want of a rider an army was lost, for want of an army a battle was lost, for want of a battle the war was lost, for want of the war the kingdom was lost, and all for the want of a little horseshoe nail.

Benjamin Franklin

Sandy's Miracle

Life isn't a matter of milestones, but moments.

Rose Kennedy

From her very beginning the little Arabian had known nothing but abuse, neglect and cruelty. Now, she was destined to die, or was she?

Lost Acres Horse Rescue, a non-profit organization for abused, neglected and injured horses had been in operation only seven weeks when the call for our fifth rescue came in. With emotions still raw after the recent death of a severe neglect case, this was a call for which we were not quite prepared.

I was baffled by the uncontrollable crying of the female caller. After several minutes of trying, I was able to calm her and learn the story of Sandy, the little fifteen-year-old Arabian mare. Sandy had been unlucky enough to be born into the ownership of a "self-made cowboy trainer" who believed that all you needed to make a good horse was a club and a few good beatings.

After several beatings for anything that he felt deserved one, the cowboy decided it was time to make Sandy a riding horse. When she refused the bit in the bridle, it called for another beating. This time, he rendered her unconscious. Shortly after this incident, Sandy was sold and now carried with her a horrible fear of men. Another home, another fear and another chapter of cruelty, this time neglect. According to her new owner, she had been riding Sandy a week before and had asked another family member to put Sandy in the barn. They did, but failed to lock her stall. Sandy opened the stall gate during the night and indulged herself in a barrel of hog feed, a natural poison to horses.

Living through something that should have certainly killed her, Sandy continued to get sicker and sicker. When she showed signs of founder, a condition causing severe pain and lameness in horses, her owner phoned the farrier and upon his recommendation, Sandy's shoes were removed. The days went by and Sandy's condition continued to worsen. As there were no large animal vets in the area, small animal vets were consulted and unfortunately, none of them were familiar with Sandy's ailment, neither the cause, condition, nor treatment. Sandy continued to grow weaker.

Unable to bear the sight of Sandy in pain any longer, Sandy's owner called her neighbor and explained the situation to him. Unable to destroy Sandy herself, she asked the neighbor if he would be willing to shoot Sandy if she went away and left a gun for him. The neighbor had heard about Lost Acres on a local TV broadcast earlier in the week and had copied our phone number. He refused to shoot Sandy, but gave her owner our number and made her promise to call us.

We arrived at Sandy's as a steady mist began to intensify. Four of us crossed a small, dusty paddock area and there, on the other side, lay the most pitiful, forlorn sight I had ever seen . . . at least since our last case. Sandy was a very small, frail, strawberry and gray Egyptian Arabian mare. Her flea-bitten coat was matted with thick dust and she lay in a fetal position capable of raising only her head.

The mist turned into a full-scale downpour as we worked

feverishly to remove part of the fence around the paddock. Sandy was unable to rise to her feet to be led to the trailer, so our only choice was to take the trailer to her. After removing the fence, we backed the trailer to where she lay and the four of us proceeded to lift her in. We laid her down and made her as comfortable as possible for the long drive home. Reina, Sandy's four-month-old foal, watched as we pulled down the drive, leaving her and taking her mother . . . somewhere.

Back at Lost Acres, we moved Sandy into a stall. With her fear of men, it proved to be a tedious task, although she did warm up to my son Dustin right away. We examined her and found her problems to be more than just founder. She was 450 pounds underweight and, as we would learn later, Sandy had been in a downed position for nearly a month. Trying to care for her foal, Sandy had used her mouth to pull herself about the paddock. In doing so, she had developed eighteen ulcerations on her body and had come in contact with an electric fence. Her tongue and lips displayed chemical and electrical burns which were proof of the fence and the use of fly spray. Sandy's reaction to the spray contracted her muscles and drew her into the fetal position in which we found her.

The next morning we began trying to help Sandy hold her head up enough so she could eat her quarter can of grain that would be given three times a day. Hay was placed in front of her to eat as she chose. Next began the task of getting her wounds cleaned and treated and to get her looking like a horse. Her coat was brushed and the mud cleaned off, quite a task with a horse lying down! With a little trimming, she began to take shape.

Three and a half weeks would pass before Sandy would be strong enough to stand on her own for fifteen minutes, three times a day to eat. One month would pass before she would be given a full can of grain at a time. Twice daily, we would work her from one side of the stall to the other so that her bedding could be cleaned.

Five weeks after Sandy arrived at Lost Acres, we were able to walk her outside her stall to stand in the aisle while her bedding was changed. As I started to take her back inside, I noticed a pool of something around her feet. Touching it revealed the beginning of another nightmare . . . blood. And a lot of it. Abscesses had formed on the inside of both her front feet. They had been deep and she had shown no signs or symptoms, but now the backs of both feet had blown out, as well as the heel bulbs on one foot. Three days later, the next of a long line of problems occured; she would lose the soles of all four feet and I would spend the next two months, two hours a day, cleaning, soaking, drenching and continuing to bandage them.

While Sandy had a terrible fear of everyone and would cower away, she would cling to me as a lifeline. She would even lie down on her side and stretch her legs out for me as I painfully cared for her feet. When we were finished, she would scoot around and cradle her head in my lap. While she was improving in some ways, I wondered if we would ever really come to the end of catastrophes. Sandy had ulcerations, four feet without soles and two feet and an elbow that had abscessed with tissue and muscle dying away. Our only good news was she was eating like a champ and the burns she had acquired from the fence and the spray were finally healed. Two months passed and while her feet were recovering, something just wasn't right. As I examined her, I discovered our next disaster. She was completely losing her front feet.

Randy, the man who would become known as our miracle farrier had seemed confident when he had told me her feet would "take some doing." I've often wondered since if he knew just how much doing. While I had always held her on a lead line for him to work with her, the time we placed her in crossties in the aisle, Sandy panicked. Only then did I realize Sandy's beatings had occurred while being held by crossties.

For the next ten months Randy painstakingly worked

with her: Trimming her feet, filling them with epoxy to help rebuild part of them, placing the right type of shoes needed for the current problem at hand. Daily, I hand-walked her for exercise and to get her adjusted to her feet. As a vet assistant for eight years, six of them with one of the best horse vets in the state of Ohio, I had acquired experience that a million dollars couldn't buy. Unfortunately, only time would tell if Sandy would make it. Fortunately, I had all the time in the world.

Sixteen months, sixteen *long* months, and the day of reckoning had arrived. For the first time, Sandy would be turned out in the large paddock without being held back by a lead line. This time she would be set free. As I walked from the paddock and turned to close the gate behind me, I heard Sandy squeal, followed by a triumphant whinny. I looked to see her standing on her hind legs, shaking her head and striking the air as if to say, "I'm back, world! I won!" She tossed her tail over her back, gave another victory squeal and ran like the wind, her mane and tail flowing like silver angel hair as she raced time and time again around the paddock. As I watched, the tears from so many months—scared tears, tears of relief, tears of joy and tears of wonder—fell to the ground. Sandy had earned her nickname, "Lost Acres' Miracle Baby."

We kept Sandy for a few more months, seeing her through to her seventeenth birthday when she was adopted as a riding horse to a wonderful home. Our policy is to supervise our adopted horses for a period of one year. We did and were elated to find Sandy was doing great. Her transition to a new home wasn't without some difficulty, but this little Arab who was destined—but refused—to die is loved like a million dollar horse and couldn't be purchased for that!

Sissy Burggraf

Wind Spirit

Courage and resolution are the spirit and soul of virtue.

Thomas Fuller

Many years ago, our friendly vet put us together with an aging couple who raised Shetland ponies. The old couple had raised a stallion from the age of three, after finding him tied to a telephone pole in a thin and ravaged condition. They brought him to their little farm, nursed him back to health and gave him a loving home for many years.

The pony was transferred to my ownership when the aged, unwell couple needed to find good homes for their small, remaining herd. Many of my friends chuckled at my decision to give the pony stallion a job on our breeding farm. From the first, Spirit earned his name. Whether Morgan or Thoroughbred mare, he rapidly became everyone's favorite. He never walked by a mare without a greeting, receiving an enthusiastic reply. Never did he exhibit a moment of disrespect to his human handlers or caretakers. Equally, he courted and mesmerized the brood mares with his throaty songs and amazing antics.

Spirit often looked much like a circus pony. He would

prance with the cadence and brilliance of a Park horse—neck erect, head and tail held high. He would leap through the air like a Lipizzaner stallion; rear on his hind legs and paw the air like the black stallion of Disney stories; or race around the paddocks to impress the brood mares like Secretariat, the famous Thoroughbred. He determined that all the mares were his mares. He of course had his favorites and would insist on being allowed to snuffle them and chat on his way out to the paddock. All the mares adored him, rushing to their stall grates with wide eyes, flared nostrils and soft, throaty nickers as he passed. Spirit was truly the King of the Barn.

He never acknowledged that his stature was not full size. His thick, long mane and tail and proud demeanor caused larger males to give way as he passed. My husband and I would joke that his glances at the other males carried a sense of aristocratic pride—almost as if he were nodding to his subjects when walking by. His harem gave him purpose. He took that responsibility seriously to heart, even to the last day.

Although aged forty-nine in October of 2004, Spirit called to his mares as he walked to the large arena. Over the last several years, he had triumphed over bouts of illness commonplace to aging horses. The stress imposed by each successive winter brought the fear that we would lose our beloved little stallion. October's cold autumn days heralded an oncoming winter of deep temperatures. Spirit tried to partner our extended care for him by rallying, but his tired body was unable to muster sufficient strength. His heart rate became dangerously high, his legs swelled with fluids, his feet became so sore as to cause him to alternately lift them while standing. He spent much time lying in his deeply bedded stall, rising to eat the small, special dietary preparations we brought several times a day. Even if lying down, he would raise his head and open his mouth to accept his medications. He tried so hard to honor our efforts to help him.

This dignified pony deserved release from the oppressive,

painful conditions he bore daily. Nothing was able to help him: not veterinary or farrier methods, not any therapy, technique, foodstuff, medication or treatment. Two nights before his last morning, I told him it was all right, time for him to leave, okay to go, and he did so with my great love and thanks. I gave him some pain relief to get him through the night. Just as I finished, he groaned and spoke to me in almost an inaudible nicker, resting his head against me, nuzzling my hand. It was as if he were saying, "I know and I love you, too."

The written word attempts to convey thought and emotion; it usually fails. How can we translate the depth of the feelings we experience, particularly with one of God's creation that does not speak the language we use to communicate with one another? When speaking with horses, I do not use English words. The horses understand me and I understand their responses, whether complaints, questions, pleasant exchanges, or loving expressions. When talking to horses, I often use English words. They have come to understand what the sounds I make mean, in terms of the actions I intend my words to effect. In turn, I understand their body language and signals, the differing tones of their vocalizing, the interpretation of their glances. The two types of communication are very different. The first, speaking with horses, is a matter of spiritual connection with another created entity. The second, talking to horses, is a matter of physical plane interaction with another species. Spirit was comfortable with and adept at communicating either way.

Standing in the arena, he gingerly lifted each of his feet, turning his head to each of us as we said our loving good-byes. Our sensitive vet injected the relieving fluid and he dropped to his rest. Because he was so small as compared to a full-sized horse, the dose administered was half the usual amount. Spirit—true to his spirited life—required the amount prescribed for a large horse before leaving his beloved, windswept farm. The inclusion of this fact is not morbid; instead, it is an indication of the strength of his character and a celebration of the greatness of his spirit. Free from pain, having said his good-byes to his herd and his humans, Wind Spirit lay at rest as beautiful in death as he was in life.

Spirit had called a bittersweet good-bye to his mares. He nobly stood, despite the pain, for his last moments with his humans. He knew he was leaving, but he intended to leave with dignity. His great strength and spirit did not fail him, even at the end. As we carried him to his final resting place on top of The Hill, the wind blew strongly, its song whispering true through the spruce trees, creating a carousel of bowing branches. I braided flowers in his glorious mane, wove buds in his forelock and tearfully kissed him one last time. All living matter eventually returns to earth's bosom in welcome continuance of life. The things of the spirit fly free with abandon to play in the wind. Wind Spirit . . . may you dance with the wind; may your majestic call find loving response from our other friends resting on The Hill. I shall think of your loud whinny, shining black body and deep, loving eyes as you rear and paw at the sky of infinity. Adieu for now . . .

Katrina L. Wood

For the Love of Racehorses

Do, or do not. There is no try.

Yoda, *Star Wars*

I stumble into my barn in the dark and cold at 4:30 in the morning, barely awake. I am greated by five heads staring out of their stall doors, listening for my footstep, looking for me to appear around the corner. Stormy blasts a whinny at me loud enough to wake the entire backstretch, then withdraws satisfied that I've arrived and his world hasn't come to an end, that his morning will now be routine. I greet them all with words and a touch; two more horses deep in their stalls barely flick an ear as I quietly slip in to unwrap their bandages and check their legs. They're like me, definitely not the cheerful early-morning types that all racehorses are rumored to be.

It'll be a busy morning. According to the training charts prepared by my trainer the previous night, all seven horses will gallop. The "Gg3/4" by Joey's name stirs my adrenaline. It's his final major work from the gate in preparation for his first start in sixteen months coming off a bowed tendon. I'm always nervous when Joey works. And, Stormy runs tonight, which means my nerves will be shot at the end of this long day. But I can't even think about that now. I have a lot of work to do in the next seven hours.

My morning is a blur. I ready my horses for riders, send them out, clean their stalls, and catch them as they return to the barn. I bathe them, hang them on the walker, water them out and watch them for stress or injuries, while getting the next horse ready for its gallop person. My layers of clothes disappear as I begin to sweat in the cool morning. My coffee gets cold as it sits untouched on a straw bale.

There's a half-hour break for the exercise riders mid-morning while the tractors smooth out the track; for me there's no time to rest. Joey will work first after the break, when the track is at its kindest, with no bumps or treacherous holes that he might stumble in at 40 mph.

I can't stand the pressure of watching, but I can't stand not to follow Joey to the track. He knows he's going to work. He knows I'm out there watching him. "Hi, Joey," I call to him as he warms up at a jog past me, "Be careful." He bows his nose to his chest and prances, his tail lifted proudly and he cocks his head toward me as he passes. I'm smitten and he knows it.

I stand apart from Joey's owner and trainer who are there with their stopwatches. From the grandstand I watch as he breaks from the gate in the chute across the track. I am terribly tense from my clenched jaw to my curled-up toes. Joey is an image of power and grace, fearsome and wondrous, floating above the track, gathering speed with every stride. He rockets around the turn into the homestretch. I try not to think of his cannon bones taking 10,000 pounds of force with every stride and those thin, fragile tendons precariously holding those bones to the muscles beneath a hurtling bullet.

As he careens toward me I shrink, try to be invisible so that my presence might not distract him. But there's no chance of that. Joey sees, hears, feels nothing but his joy of running. I'm overwhelmed by the tension, the excitement, the beauty, the raw power of my beast, when I sense something wrong. I glance to the finish line and my heart stops. A riderless horse is galloping full speed on the rail, toward Joey.

I am frozen to my spot; I can do nothing but watch. It's all a blur, happening too fast, though everything feels like it's in slow motion. Too late, I scream, *"LOOSE HORSE!"* but they don't hear me. Joey is running on instinct. The rider's head is buried in Joey's mane. Forty yards apart, the rider sees approaching disaster. She stands up on Joey and tries to slow him, but there's no stopping a bullet.

A miracle happens. The loose horse swerves around Joey right before they collide. I about faint on the spot. My horse has still turned in the bullet work for the day at six furlongs.

Joey is very pleased with himself as he cools out, no concept of his near-death. I can't forget what just happened, can't stop my knees from shaking as I finish cleaning stalls and begin grooming my horses and massaging muscles and icing legs and applying standing bandages. My fingers tremble as I inspect Joey's legs, feeling his tendons and suspensory ligaments, searching for heat or the slightest swelling. But his legs are cold and tight. My trainer confirms his soundness before I apply a cool poultice.

The exercise riders are done for the day by 10:30. I am finished close to noon and I have a few hours break until the second half of my day begins. I grab a lunch and fall asleep on the couch in our office until my alarm goes off at 3:30.

Chore time; pick stalls, water and feed the starving beasts—each of which insists he or she is the hungriest horse in the barn and wants to be fed first. It takes a little diplomacy and bribery and sneaking around to make my seven horses all think each of them was the most deserving one who got fed first.

Stormy's not hungry—he knows he's running. He's in the seventh race, which on this weeknight means he won't enter the starting gate until 8:30. Stormy is on Lasix, so once the vet arrives to give him his shot at 4:30, I can't leave the barn. I settle down with a book to wait the hours out and try to concentrate on the words and not think about the race coming up. Stormy takes the wait much better; he stands in the back of his stall, dozing, saving up his emotions for the race.

Stormy had his bath in the morning and he absolutely hates being brushed, so all I have to do is run a soft rag containing baby oil and alcohol over his coat to make it shine. I comb a checkerboard pattern on his butt and tie one small braid in his mane for good luck. At the ten-minute call for the seventh race I rinse out his mouth with a syringe full of water and I run his bandages and bridle him. The only things betraying his coolness are his huge eyes and the occasional tremors that run through his muscles.

I lead Stormy to the paddock where his trainer awaits us for saddling. His owners are there also, expecting a big win. They won't get it because Stormy's in over his head again. They want him to be an allowance horse, so they insist he run in allowance races, even though he will never be quite that good. This will be the last time my trainer humors them.

Even though we have no shot tonight, as I watch my handsome horse warm up on the track, I'm terribly nervous. He will try his hardest because he knows I'm watching and because he has the biggest heart in the world. I am so lucky to have this horse, and in fact, the seven most gorgeous horses on the planet to take care of, no matter how fast they run.

Stormy looks good for the first half-mile, keeping his blinkered head and white nose in front until the eighth pole, where the better horses pass him. But he hangs tough and will not give up and is only beaten by four lengths. He looks for me as he returns in front of the stands to be unsaddled. I notice his back heels are raw from running down through his bandages. There are welts on his flank where the whip lashed him—as if he hadn't been giving his all in the last stages of the race.

With an arm draped over his neck, I tell him how proud of him I am as we carry our battle scars on the long walk back to our barn. His owners arrive and stand around with hands on hips, watching their investment, a bit disappointed again, no praise for his intense efforts; ready again with all but the one correct excuse for him tonight—he was over-matched. Stormy ignores his owners, nickers to me from the walker for a drink of water, for reassurance, to let me know he's cooled out and wants to stop walking in circles.

It's just Stormy and me left; his owners and trainer are long gone. I doctor his "owies" and bandage his front legs. It's getting late, but Stormy and I can't resist sneaking off to a meticulously landscaped grassy area that's off-limits to horses and humans. I figure he deserves a treat after tonight's great effort.

By the time I hang Stormy's feed tub, it's almost midnight. It's been a long day, I'm physically tired and mentally worn out and I have a half-hour drive home. Even so, I can't wait to hear Stormy's good morning nicker five hours from now and to do it all over again.

Merri Melde

Class and Courage

To be hopeful in bad times is not just foolishly romantic. It is based on the fact that human history is a history not only of cruelty but also of compassion, sacrifice, courage, kindness.

Howard Zinn

I rode up the center line of the dressage arena and saluted the judge with more confidence than I'd ever felt in a show ring. Yes, I'd memorized and practiced the training level test, but more important, I totally trusted my mount and my chestnut Thoroughbred mare trusted me. She stood quietly beneath me—calm, but alert—and eager to do her job. In less than a year of working together, we'd bonded to the point of knowing each other's every move. The unfamiliar surroundings and crisp winter weather today did not make Brenda nervous, only a little sharper. She expected this to be fun and so did I.

We moved through the test easily, executing every change of gait at the right spot, picking up the correct leads and staying on the bit. Brenda lacked that extra bit of energy, or "impulsion," that dressage judges prize, but no one could overlook her perfect obedience or willing attitude. That day, we beat out every competitor in our class but one and took second place.

To me, that red ribbon meant as much as a blue. This was the kind of rapport I'd always hoped to feel with a horse. I'd been equine-crazy all my life, but not until well into middle age had I been able to afford even this "half-a-horse" by sharing ownership of Brenda with my trainer.

I can't say I fell in love with Brenda at first sight. When she arrived at the boarding stable on consignment, her ribs and hipbones stuck out, her ragged mane flopped over her skinny neck in both directions at once and her back showed dark, balding patches. Her papers gave her age as twelve, but she looked older. She'd come from a rundown stable where she'd worked as a lesson and trail horse. The former owner explained Brenda was allergic to hay and had been fed silage, a kind of cattle feed, instead.

The first time I rode Brenda I was amazed by her game attitude. She moved with easygoing energy and the minute I asked, she gave me a passable leg yield and shoulder-in. My trainer didn't want to sell her, but neither of us could afford the rather outrageous asking price. So, we decided to share her.

It soon became clear that Brenda suffered from Chronic Obstructive Pulmonary Disorder, commonly known as heaves. She actually seemed to be allergic to summer pollen and although she could eat hay, it had to be rinsed of all dust. She suffered most when confined to a stall. On the vet's recommendations, we kept her outdoors round-the-clock and gave her supplements to build up her strength.

Under this regimen, Brenda did well for several months. She gained 200 much-needed pounds and her coat improved. We pulled her mane and trimmed her tail to make her presentable for showing.

I schooled her in dressage, visiting the stable about three times a week. Through grooming her and hanging out while she grazed in her field, I fell in love with her. Most horses I'd dealt with before could be classified as either smart and

energetic but high-strung, or calm and reliable but a bit bor-
ing. Brenda was close to bomb-proof, yet she noticed everything around her and learned quickly—in hand or under
saddle, she was good company. What's more, she radiated a
gentle spirit that impressed everyone who dealt with her. On
one of the scorecards I collected after a dressage test, the
judge had written, "Sweet horse!"

She bonded strongly with one gelding at a time, seeming
to need a boyfriend. If that horse left the stable, she'd soon
become joined at the hip with another. She could even
empathize with another horse in trouble, once stopping in
the middle of a training session and whinnying in protest
because she'd seen an equine friend being corrected with a
smack from a riding crop.

During her second summer with me, Brenda's health
worsened. After even mild exercise, she labored for breath,
her nostrils huge and her lungs visibly heaving behind her
ribs. We put her on steroids to open up her lung passages and
hoped that as fall approached her allergies would ease as
they had the previous year. But this time she stayed sicker
for longer. That September, only a few months after we'd
won that red ribbon, she struggled to perform for me in
another dressage show. As usual, she did everything I asked,
but at the final halt she was breathing so hard I feared she
might collapse. Feeling terrible for having put her under such
a strain, I scratched her from her second class, sponged her
down and trailered her back to the barn.

My trainer moved her operations to a stable in the next
town, where things went from bad to worse. Brenda could no
longer be left outside at night because of the threat of bears
in the area. She was fed with a group of other horses and the
stablehand wasn't about to wash all of the hay, so she
inhaled dust particles that aggravated her condition. For a
while I still tried to ride her in the ring and she'd start out
eagerly, but after only a few minutes she'd end up gasping
for air. She dropped weight again until she looked as bad as
when I'd first seen her.

I still came to the stable three times a week to groom her and hand-walk her so she could graze. Brenda always greeted me with a gleam in her eye and a spring in her step, having no idea how sick she was. Her situation was her situation and she accepted it bravely. Alone with her in the stable aisle, I'd run the brush over her skeletal ribs and listen to her struggle for breath, tears running down my face. I'd hug her neck and whisper to her, "I'll get you out of here, I promise!"

I bought my trainer out of her share of Brenda and moved the mare to another stable where she could have a shed row stall for maximum ventilation. The vet at the new farm recommended a senior feed that helped her regain some weight and the stable help faithfully rinsed her hay. She recovered to the point where I could ride her a little, but I feared her useful days already were behind her and I worried about what that would mean. On the meager income of a freelance writer, I couldn't afford paying for her full board and heavy-duty medications much longer.

The owner at the new stable suggested gently that it might be time to put her down, but I couldn't reconcile myself to that. With the right care, Brenda could still enjoy life. Turned loose in a paddock, she still loved to gallop, even though she quickly became exhausted. She had the heart of a Thoroughbred, after all. If she refused to give up on life, how could I give up on her?

I found a wonderful farm in Pennsylvania that took horses with problems. If they could be rehabilitated they'd be offered for adoption, but if no one wanted them they could stay at the farm. This last part was important to me. I suspected no one would want to adopt a very sick, unrideable mare. And I couldn't risk letting Brenda go to a home where they might eventually give up on her and send her off to slaughter.

I phoned Beverlee Dee of Bright Futures Farm and she sympathized with my dilemma. We agreed she would take Brenda and I'd send a monthly sum to cover her medication.

I cried the day Beverlee loaded Brenda into her van, but only because I was losing a dear friend. I felt sure Beverlee would take good care of her.

Brenda settled in comfortably, though she followed her usual pattern of suffering through the summer weather and improving dramatically in the winter. She also continued to charm everyone who dealt with her and of bonding with a special boyfriend—in this case, another Thoroughbred named Shifter.

After a few months, the arthritis in Brenda's legs worsened and she developed a septic hock that needed surgery. Beverlee, who had also been inspired by the chestnut mare's unflagging spirit, believed she could overcome this setback and like me, was willing to go the extra mile to give Brenda a chance. The operation at Ohio State University Veterinary Hospital was a success and Brenda returned to Bright Futures and Shifter, on all four legs. The following summer her heaves grew so severe that we worried she might not make it to the fall, but were relieved when her allergies subsided and she started to regain her winter weight. We nursed Brenda from one health crisis to another and she never failed to amaze us at her resilience and love of life.

To help ease her heaves, Brenda spent nights out in the pasture with several other horses, including Shifter. One November morning Beverlee called the horses into the barn for breakfast. They all came, except for Shifter and Brenda. Shifter, his warm breath visible in the cold morning air, stood out in the pasture, guarding Brenda's lifeless body. From marks found on her blanket it was apparent Shifter had made a valiant effort to help Brenda to her feet, but she had died of a heart attack during the night.

True to her noble spirit, Brenda had spared us from ever having to make the decision to end her life. Instead, she died out in the pasture as she had lived her life, with class and courage, her last boyfriend close by, no doubt just the way she would have wanted to go.

Eileen Watkins

Dirty Trick

My pony likes the curry comb
To scratch across his back,
To itch those places that had been
Underneath the tack.

I brush away the dirt and mud,
The grass and shedding hair.
I brush and brush and brush some more
With tender loving care.

But when I put him in the ring
He drops and rolls around,
His feet kick up into the air
As he squirms upon the ground.

He's filthy now when he stands up
And needs another brush
Which makes me think my pony likes
His curry comb too much!

Lawrence Schimel

Angels in Winter

*We are each of us angels with only one wing
and we can only fly by embracing one another.*
                                    Luciano de Crescenzo

It was a beautiful winter morning. Several feet of fresh snow had fallen the night before and the crisp air cooled my lungs when I drew in a breath. As I drove to the barn where I stabled my sister's horse, the tree branches strained beneath the heavy snow, creating a glistening tunnel across the road. The sun was just coming up over the hills . . . it was going to be a perfect winter day in Ohio.

I greeted my trainer, Kathy, and walked out to the field where Jordan had been turned out with her pasture friend, Tinkerbelle. Kathy and I have been trainer and student, mentor and friends for the past eleven years. Today we had planned an early lesson so that I could get home to my four-year-old before my husband left for work.

Having just been turned out, the horses were not eager to come inside. The field they were in was mostly wooded and surrounded by fencing on three sides with a lake on the fourth. Being January, the lake had long been frozen and it created a scenic natural barrier to the pasture. Kathy and I walked together with grain, calling the girls, laughing at their naughtiness.

At the sound of our voices and lured by the promise of grain, Jordan stopped trotting around, but Tink continued goofing off. As we watched helplessly, Tinkerbelle ventured out onto the icy lake. Jordan, no longer distracted by our calls, began to walk gingerly behind her. We stared in horror at Tinkerbelle, nearly fifty feet from the bank, and Jordan not far behind her. Kathy and I stood motionless desperately calling for them to come back. To our relief, Tinkerbelle began to turn when suddenly the ice gave way beneath her, plunging her entire body into the lake, only her head above the ice. Almost simultaneously, the ice broke beneath Jordan and she too was submerged in the frigid water.

Without speaking, Kathy ran to the barn to call for help, while I ran to the horses. Both horses struggled to get out, their hooves breaking the three-inch thick ice in front of them as it gave way time and time again. Tinkerbelle kept trying to rear, to get above the ice, to no avail. Kathy arrived with halters and I very carefully made my way out to each horse, haltering them. Together, we started with Tinkerbelle, pulling as hard as we could to get her to move forward toward the bank. Jordan began neighing, trying to come toward us and away from the bank.

Leaving Tink to Kathy, I turned my attention to Jordan to get her turned in the right direction and began trying to coax her out. Both mares had heavy winter blankets on that quickly filled with icy water, making their efforts even more difficult from the excessive weight. Tink and Jordan were tiring and starting to give up. It had been ten minutes since they fell through and the freezing temperature was taking its toll.

We turned at the sound of a truck to see our blacksmith, Jason, running towards us. He and Kathy spoke quickly and he ran for the tractor. Seconds later, the fire department arrived and began to assess the situation. Jason backed the tractor to the lake, looked at me and asked, "Which one?" I never felt so helpless in all my life. Tinkerbelle was still fighting to get out, but Jordan had gone into shock and was slipping beneath the water. With tears in my eyes, I pointed at Tinkerbelle, hoping that we could keep Jordan's head above water until they got Tink out. It took almost ten minutes for Tinkerbelle to be drug out by the tractor. She had been in the lake for over half an hour.

One of Kathy's resourceful neighbors had a friend with an ice saw. Tom arrived and began cutting the ice in front of Jordan. In shock, she had stopped struggling and lay floating on her side in the frigid water. Every time the tractor would pull, her legs would get caught underneath the thick ice. Without a thought, Tom waded into the freezing water and cut a path in the ice all the way to the bank allowing us to drag Jordan, on her side, out of the lake.

Once on the bank, we cut Jordan's blankets off and tried to get her up. She wouldn't move. Everyone pushed and pulled until we were able to get her to her feet. With me leading her and someone holding her tail we made it into the miniature horse barn. We grabbed every blanket, wool cooler and anti-sweat sheet we could find and piled them onto each horse. We massaged their legs, tried to keep them moving and waited for the vet.

When Tinkerbelle emerged from the lake, her temperature was only 96 degrees and Jordan's was a dangerous 92 degrees, nearly ten degrees below normal. Larry, our farm vet, arrived with his technician, Deb, and they quickly went to work. Jordan was in bad shape. She was still in shock and Larry wasn't sure she would make it. He began working on her while Deb worked with Tink. They set up IVs and started warm fluids. Deb and Larry pumped their stomachs with warm mineral oil and water, administered antibiotics and several other medicines.

Tinkerbelle's temperature began to rise quickly and she showed marked improvement within an hour. Jordan was slower to respond, but her temp began to climb ever so slowly. Once they were stablized, we moved Jordan and

Tink to the larger barn to their own stalls, gingerly making our way down the drive. We watched both of them closely for any signs of distress over the next two weeks and miraculously both horses recovered with no complications, not even a cold.

Without the generosity, bravery and quick thinking of everyone who responded to Kathy's call, we surely would have two less horses today. I have never been able to adequately express my gratitude and appreciation to the angels that came to our rescue that morning. Every nuzzle and whinny from Tinkerbelle and Jordan remind me I must live each day trying to make a difference in someone else's life. That is the best thank you I can offer.

Therese Evans

The Fifty-Cent Ride

Life is what happens, after you make other plans.

Ralph Marston

"Big," whispered my tiny three-year-old granddaughter as she gazed up at the palomino Quarter Horse. She clutched her mother's knee and hesitantly reached out to touch the mare. The horse's nicker and swish of tail caused her to giggle. Her delight reminded me of her mother. I was awash with memories.

"We want to ride a horse," our five-year-old twin daughters begged repeatedly on a trip to Colorado. Never mind that none of us had been closer to a horse than a carousel, TV, or a movie screen. Seeing a hand-painted sign for trail rides, we decided to indulge them just once. The rancher led us to what looked like a tired, old brown horse.

"She's my calmest mare. You can lead her around that circular path over there." He pointed past an ancient oak tree to a clearing of dirt and scrub pines. "Let your little girls take turns while you keep hold of the reins," he advised, then added, "That'll be fifty cents."

It was the most expensive fifty cents we ever spent.

We gave him two quarters and started our walk, each of our daughters having a turn in the saddle. They were enthralled and talked of nothing else on the entire trip home to California.

"Can we take lessons?" they asked constantly in the weeks that followed.

"We'll see." I said, evading their question, "Let's go to dance class first."

"Okay. But then can we ride?"

"We'll talk to Daddy." Fortunately, he was out of town.

So they began six weeks of ballet classes and enjoyed them. Still, the constant quest was to ride again. I hoped their passion for horses would pass.

"You need to try gymnastics, first." I told them.

"Why?"

"Well . . ." I stammered as I struggled for an answer to our persistent little girls, "you just need to learn about balance and stuff."

They stared at me, nodded and together said, "*Then* can we ride horses?"

"We'll see." My standby answer was becoming a little weak.

Gymnastics was less of a hit than dance. Why could they sit so straight and tall in a saddle high on a horse's back, yet a stationary balance beam caused such fear they clung to it with both arms and legs like a panther to a tree limb? They were not charmed. Months passed as I dragged them to swimming and then tennis lessons and on to art and piano. They learned, but without great enthusiasm, always asking, "When can we ride?"

We finally found a stable with rental horses and lessons. I assumed they'd tire of riding in a few weeks as they had their other classes. No such luck. The girls spent rainy weeks learning how to groom the horses, climbing up on stools to brush them, lifting each leg and bracing it between their own as they picked hooves. They learned to hold their hands flat when they offered apple treats. Too small to bridle and saddle, they watched the grooms with rapt interest and quickly learned.

Rainy season passed, the sun came out and at last, it was time to ride. They were given a leg up and each sat high atop a horse's back. *They look so tiny up there*, I thought. Clicking their tongues and tightening their legs as they'd been instructed, they moved forward into the arena, eyes shining, mouths in tentative smiles of pride and excitement. They seemed completely and naturally at home there. I shook my head and knew we were in for a long ride.

Within months, one of our daughters fell off her runaway horse. Bruises and scrapes covered her small body and her sister was pale and wide-eyed from watching. A call to the doctor was soon followed by a trip to the hospital and emergency surgery for a ruptured spleen. Our little girl had not only fallen off the horse, she had fallen under it. After an interminable hour, the surgeon walked toward us with a smile on his face, assuring us our daughter would be fine. "Can you guess what her first words in the recovery room were?" We shook our heads. "She gazed up at me and whispered, 'When can I ride?'"

"Never!" I uttered, without even thinking.

"Oh, you have to let her ride again—her sister, too. Don't forget that old saying," the doctor reminded us, "when you fall from a horse you should get right on again."

They were soon back on horses, those of their own—a palomino Quarter Horse and a chestnut Thoroughbred. The girls rode well and entered local horse shows, serving as grooms for each other. It was a world apart from any we had ever known and as the years flew by we enjoyed the camaraderie and family togetherness. There were the 4 a.m. wake-ups, special baths and braiding for the horses, unique outfits and hair styles for the girls, hours driving to the arenas, dirt and sweat, frustration and work. But mostly there was the joy.

Our daughters were enthralled with every aspect of riding. It was a beautiful sight to see them ride, to watch as they became part of their horses' flowing motions, lost in subtle communication and concentration. It became obvious that they had special gifts and inborn passion. They would have found their way to horses even if we hadn't opened the door long ago with that fifty-cent ride.

"Nana, look at me!" Our granddaughter sat high on the golden mare, her arms relaxed and her legs spread wide with her toes tucked in as she balanced perfectly.

The vision brought me full circle. As with our daughters, her enchantment was there, the beginning of full-grown passion. I looked up at her and took her hand while her mother gently led us around the arena. Here we go again, I thought and this time, I smiled.

Jean Stewart

On My Left Side

To live fully is to let go and die with each pass-ing moment and to be reborn in each new one.

Jack Kornfield

I was so filled with a lifetime's wait that I could hardly believe it when he appeared at the top of the ramp, wide-eyed and snorting. He paused long enough to rip a mouth-ful of hay from a swinging haybag and then, chewing, followed the driver down the ramp, carefully picking his way onto solid ground. He was dark and lean, shining coat over sinew and fine bone.

I took the lead and smoothed his neck while I crooned a hello. My world narrowed to a pinhole encircling only him and me. He paced, circled me restlessly and then froze to stare at the horizon. He stretched his topline and flexed his cordoned hip muscles. He was elegant, breathtaking. He rocked forward on his toes. And he peed. He let forth a froth-ing stream he must have been holding for hundreds of miles. He groaned with relief as I giggled and stepped aside. The spell was broken. He was here and he was real.

His name was Maybe and he had come to me through a series of kindnesses following an endless wait. A lifetime of riding other people's horses, years of university study and an eon of filling a seat in the bleachers as a horseless horsewoman.

As a racehorse Maybe was forgettable but as a hunter he showed phenomenal promise. Our first rides proved he was green but levelheaded. The next few months revealed he was also occasionally bullheaded. There were times when I'd squeeze Maybe to ask for a trot and he'd lock up. No problem, I would think, I'll just ask again. Cluck, cluck, kick. Still nothing—he wouldn't move except to pin his ears. More kicks meant nothing except more pinned ears.

Kick.

Pin.

Kick!

Pin!

Kick, Kick!

PIN!

And so we would stay, motionless in the middle of the arena, arguing and blocking traffic while I decided how best to move 1,100 pounds of stubbornness. Half the time I didn't know whether to laugh or howl with frustration.

I reveled in the way people gravitated toward him; they would pick him out of a crowd to pet him and say how beautiful he was. Maybe relished nakedness and wrinkled his face halfway up his nose when I approached with a sheet or blanket. He loved treats with wild abandon. Apples, carrots and especially peppermints all met their fate with a shattering crunch and enthusiastic drooling. When I walked with Maybe, he would slip behind to my left side and touch my swinging hand with his nose. Just barely, just enough for me to feel his silk against my palm. Just enough for me to sense his love and happiness at sharing a quiet moment together.

I guarded my time with Maybe and took great pride in his accomplishments. At the barn I didn't chat with other boarders, didn't hang out in the aisle; instead, I got to know my horse and became his friend. I scratched his ears just right, sang to him softly and took him to graze. He learned to lunge, to drive, to ride quietly and follow his nose. We labored over transitions and groundpoles and I learned along with him. Finally, we began to jump. He loved it. His boldness made him trustworthy, his talent made him good and his magnetism drew admirers.

I imagined him at some future show, walking out of the lineup to receive a ribbon. I envisioned him old and sway-backed in a pasture out my back door, waiting at the fence for treats. I was wrong. He died suddenly and violently, in an accident that ripped the life from him so fast it left him without pain. It left me without breath, without comprehension, without reason. I was strong but losing Maybe brought me to my knees. I moved in a fog for days. I couldn't fill all the empty hours without him and I felt . . . unraveled. Aimless. Intensely lonely. Still, I got out of bed every day and went to work. I traveled and cleaned the house. I made donations in Maybe's memory and walked my dog. It was a long and very dark winter.

Spring found me better. I couldn't often smile about him or talk of him casually, but I had made my peace with Maybe's going. I was thinking about riding again and then a call came from my trainer, Leslie. She had chosen Maybe for me and she had cried with me when he died. Now she wanted me to visit and tell her what I thought of a horse.

I went to Idaho feeling distant and unemotional through two airports and a two-hour drive. But when I got to Leslie's house, I hugged her extra tight—so much had happened since I last saw her. We walked into the barn and standing there was a horse named Sam. He was skinny, tall and sweet, not long over a career in racing. I said hello to him. I put his blanket on and noticed he did not object to his clothes. The next two days I rode Sam and talked about Maybe. On the third day, I said I would like to have Sam. It was time and Sam seemed right.

Eight months to the day that Maybe died, I answered an early morning phone call. It was the shippers. They were on their way to Sam's new barn. By the time I got to the barn

Sam was already in a stall. He stood quietly, wearing Maybe's sheet and halter. Wearing Maybe's shipping wraps. All of it was now his: He was my second horse.

I said hello to Sam and took off his sheet, took off his halter, took off his wraps. I made sure he was whole and brushed every inch of him. He was perfect and warm, with a rumbling belly unhurriedly filling with grass hay. He politely accepted carrots and ate them in miniscule bites. He chewed with his mouth closed, in what seemed a perfect nod to his proper British bloodlines. This veneer cracked when I forced him to eat electrolyte paste. I pushed it to the back of his mouth and he did his best to spit it out. Finally swallowed, the paste left a smear on his lips and a mark on our relationship. For the next ten minutes, Sam gave me the cold shoulder. He sniffed a treat in my hand and then turned his head decisively away. I was no longer trustworthy. When my boyfriend offered the same treat, Sam promptly ate it with an appreciative nibble and nuzzle. Eventually, I was able to coax him into taking another treat and he reluctantly found it acceptable.

Today Sam greets me affectionately and makes me chuckle with his dry sense of humor. He makes me proud with his willingness to work hard and learn quickly. He does not pin his ears or wrinkle his face as Maybe did. He chooses different fights and different pleasures. Sam is a quieter soul, without a hint of Maybe's reckless exuberance. I love him differently because he is different.

I am certain Maybe would have loved playing with Sam and hated sharing me with him. Sometimes, as I walk with Sam on my right, I swear I can feel Maybe on my left, just barely touching my swinging palm with his silky nose.

Katie Reynolds

A Work of Art

*Life is a great big canvas and you should throw
all the paint on it you can.*

Danny Kaye

I guess it all started when my dad rode a horse into the bar
on the Fourth of July. My brother and I were eleven and ten at
the time and we were thrilled that our father was part of our
small, hometown parade. Dad was a horseman, a clown in the
rodeo and full of spirit. He rode bareback, galloping up the
main drag in the parade. When he got to the intersection, he
placed that horse in a controlled rear, and then rode him up
three brick steps and into the bar. Dad ordered a shot and a
beer and the horse got a pretzel. We already thought our dad
was the greatest, but now he was *so cool.*

As a child, I was a dancer on the Tony Grant's Stars of
Tomorrow Show. For two weeks almost every summer I performed up to five shows daily in Atlantic City, New Jersey,
home of the Steel Pier and my next vivid memory of a horse. In
a phenomenal feat of showmanship, the pier's famous Diving
Horse and a tiny young woman, clad in nothing more than a
swimsuit and helmet, would dive bareback from a platform
thirty feet in the air.

The horse would surface and walk up the ramp with the female daredevil still on his back and stand proudly while the rider removed her helmet, flinging her long, blonde hair in the salt-air breeze. The crowd would go wild and without fail, horse and rider were greeted by an elderly lady holding a bucket filled with carrots. I carefully scheduled my free time between my own performances to watch these exciting dives. The horses were fearless and the girls that rode the horses were my absolute idols. It was an exciting show that cemented my respect and awe for these powerful creatures.

Many years later, I ended up in Truckee, California, where I founded the Truckee Ballet and I was ready for a horse of my own. I remembered what my father always told me, "If you ever get a horse, get a Quarter Horse," and I planned on doing just that. "Well-broke, five-year-old gelding Buckskin Quarter Horse Mustang 15.2-hands, $1,200," the ad read. The cowboys had named him Cholla after one of the worst things in the desert, the cholla cactus. He followed me instantly, without the lead line and let me groom him and pick up his feet. The rancher explained Cholla was eighteen months old when they gelded him and that he was proud-cut. They broke him by sacking him out; a cruel, but common process. I can't imagine what a fight that was, but I know Cholla has never forgotten it. A few days later, the rancher delivered Cholla and the relationship between a novice horse owner and a time-bomb of a horse began.

Owning a sacked-out mustang is fraught with trials and tribulations. In the beginning, he hated any kind of rope, forceful men, trailers, horseshoers—the list was a long one. Gradually, I was able talk him through fearful situations. His intelligence now tells him that he is well taken care of and capable of trust. I'd like to say that I trust *him* completely, but I can't quite say that. Cholla shows love and trust toward me, but he is fearless—ready to explode into instinctive survival mode at any time. But his equine attributes pale in comparison to his most appealing and amazing talent.

One day I was painting the corral fence with Cholla following right with me, step-by-step. Watching the procession, my husband called out, "Why don't you get that horse to paint the fence?" so I tacked a piece of paper to the fence and showed Cholla one stroke. To our amazement and delight, he understood. Yes, Cholla paints—and not fences. His medium is watercolor and he paints at his easel holding an artist's brush with his teeth. What's more, he loves doing it. What's better, he's actually good at it. When he sees me bringing the easel he licks and paws in excited anticipation. His greatest limitation—the lack of opposable thumbs—requires that I put the paint on the brush before Cholla takes it from me, but once loaded, Cholla goes straight to his easel. He may not choose the color, but Cholla decides where that color is going to go. With very deliberate and precise strokes, he creates images that are one of a kind. I've seen him roll the brush in his teeth to create a beautiful stroke. Other than loading the brush with paint, no one assists Cholla with his art. No one rotates the paper or moves the easel while Cholla is painting. His creations are his.

Cholla's talent has gained him international notoriety. His work is shown in galleries and purchased by collectors. He has been profiled in horse magazines and his art was featured when I appeared as a guest on *MARTHA*. I presented Martha Stewart with a framed original that Cholla had painted the day she was released from Alderson. It is abstract, but the image of a horse drinking champagne is quite clear and Martha recognized this, asking the audience, "Do you see it?" She showed her appreciation with a parting gift of watercolors and brushes for Cholla.

As a dancer, I know that art manifests itself as we create and that the more one's creativity is acknowledged, the more it develops—be it man or beast. I cannot explain Cholla's desire, let alone his ability, to express himself by painting. Is his work the manifestation of the essence of other artists or a physic premonition, or an ancestral memory? I cannot say. But if someday, I find him practicing pliés at the barre in his stall, I'm calling Martha!

Renee Chambers

Finding My Way Home

To know after absence the familiar street and road and village and house is to know again the satisfaction of home.

Hal Borland

I sit on horseback at the top of a hill formed out of rock and sagebrush, looking over the valley that was my home for the first eighteen years of my life. It was by this valley I learned directions, big mountains—East, little mountains—West. Behind me the foothills of the Oquirrh Mountains begin (the little mountains). The bigger range, the Rockies, rise across the valley from me, their tips still covered in snow in this early June.

As I stand contemplating the panoramic view, my horse impatiently steps in place underneath me, slightly jostling me up and down. With each jostle the saddle moans and the smell of dust fills my nostrils. My horse is a Morgan and they have little patience for standing still. His coat is the color of dark chocolate. The white on his face bleeds around his eye in a large star that goes down his face into a strip. On his body he has only one small streak of white in his mane. I envy his wavy mane and tail; my own brown hair falls straight.

I pat his neck, "Easy, little man."

He came to us with the name Coone, but I call him this only around others or when I'm angry with him.

I've explored most of these hills, all on him. We've been shot at by careless target shooters, found fresh cougar tracks, watched the flames of a forest fire dance in the dark, been lost and nearly tumbled down the shear cliff of a steep ravine numerous times. And yet since I turned twelve, I couldn't be kept from these hills.

When we first moved here my dad wouldn't allow me to ride outside the yard alone. He was afraid of my getting hurt and not being able to get help, and rightly so. Slowly though I talked him into allowing me to go up our dirt lane to the mailboxes, then I begged to go as far as the canal, which is the barrier between the hills and our town. By the time I was thirteen I had no boundaries. I rode everywhere. Coone was the only horse I trusted enough to go alone. It was my time to be alone.

Standing on these foothills looking over my home gives me the opportunity to look over my life. Problems just look smaller here. Coone and I make a good pair—he likes to hike and I don't. But both of us love to see what's beyond the next rise.

He's how I survived my teens. On the days I simply needed to escape my problems, I would drop the reins and push Coone to run and run he did. I would have to remember sunglasses to keep the gnats from slapping my face and sticking to my contacts. Those runs were my salvation.

During my senior year in high school, I spent a lot of time up here looking over my life. It was time to leave home. My oldest brother was married December of that year and my other brother was about to be engaged. It had always been the three of us. But at home I was still someone's little girl, or someone's little sister; I couldn't become anything else. I was seventeen. I knew it was time to leave, to grow up and become whoever it was I was going to become. Those that love you the most never allow you to change.

One summer day that year, I felt claustrophobic in my life. I was working in a dark hardware store, where the ten-foot shelves blocked out the sun from the one window. I was going to school until noon and working until eight, desperate to save enough for college. It was 9:30 that night before I was done with chores and free to do what I wanted. The light was barely grasping the hills when I caught my horse and fumbled with the saddle as I raced the sun. My dad caught me.

"You're not going riding, it's too late."

"I have to go, Dad. I won't be very late."

He and my stepmom were leaving for the night and begged me to be careful and come home before absolute darkness set in.

I rushed into the hills, and at the first flat trail I found, I dropped the reins and pushed the horse into a run. Faster and faster we went, with my hands stretched in the air and the cold wind blowing my hair back. The darkness hid the trail ahead of us and I trusted my horse to find the path. I tasted the cold dust on my tongue, the same flavor as the night. It was well past 11:00 when I pulled the saddle off and called it a night. It was dark enough to see the sparks kicked up from Coone's horseshoes.

It was around April when I found out my chance to leave had come. I had picked up the mail on my way home from the hills. I sat on my horse in the driveway staring at the envelope with the return address of Utah State University staring back. Trembling, I opened it. "We are pleased to inform you, that you have received a full tuition scholarship to Utah State University."

As much as I loved those hills and that horse, I knew I would have to leave them. A two-hour drive may not seem like a faraway college, but in my family we considered my brother living on the other side of the freeway long distance.

My freshman year was difficult. My roommates ostracized me for being different from them. Now, daily, I felt claustrophobic in my life. I would run on foot until I reached a rise so I could see the sun setting over the Cache Valley foothills and smell the farms below me. One night I walked until midnight, missing the horse that had carried me.

After a few years, it was time to go even further. I went to west Texas for a year and a half. I grew to love the people that inhabited that treeless plain, but I never fully felt at ease.

At the end of eighteen months, I sat on a plane bringing me back to my valley. We began our final descent above my snow-covered hills. I pressed my face against the double-paned window and traced with my finger the many trails I had ridden. I was almost home. In a matter of seconds we crossed over trails that had taken me years to explore. We were low enough that I could make out the landmarks that pointed toward home.

I had only one ride in those hills before I returned to college to complete my senior year. Finally enough time and distance had passed that I could be comfortable with who I am.

My life has circled back to these hills. Coone steps underneath me, though he's not as antsy as he used to be. He's getting old, when I drop the reins the fastest we go is a canter. I feel his age with each stiff step he takes. I'm as picky with horses as I am with people. I just don't bond with very many. While Coone had a wild streak and tendency to scare easily, I never felt fear on him. I knew he would never hurt me and never leave me. He's why I could ride so long and so far by myself. It will be difficult to find something else to ride after he's, . . . but I choose not to think that far ahead.

The houses of the valley now surround my hills like waves against the cliff. I feel their presence like I feel Coone's age. I stare at them, slightly amused. They're in for a surprise when the fire season starts. Twice I've watched flames run down the hills toward our home. Both times it was only stopped by the canal. Now those homes have jumped the canal.

The only job I could find after I graduated from college

was farther away from Coone than I had hoped. I live in the city, a step away from everything but peace. Now when I ride I'm consumed with thoughts of ways to come home instead of how to leave it. I think I finally went far enough to find a way back, back to my horse and back to my hills.

Melissa Dymock

A Friend Like No Other

Destiny is not a matter of chance; it is a matter of choice. It is not a thing to be waited for; it is a thing to be achieved.

William Jennings Bryan

Tigress came into my life just when I needed her most. That was in 1967 when I was a shy, intense fourteen-year-old, the only late-blooming ugly duckling among the five girls in my family. My sisters, two older and two younger, were all pretty and popular, with friends in the right circles and boyfriends to spare. I, the tallest and most freckled, had crooked teeth, thick glasses and red hair. My friends were the out crowd, a fact I tried to hide from my mother, herself a lifelong beauty. My family assured me that I, too, was attractive but a simple glance in the mirror proved otherwise.

Things would look up for me at sixteen. That's when the braces came off, the contact lenses went in and my long, straight hair proved perfect for the times. By then though, it was almost a moot point. Something else had already ridden to my rescue, two years earlier. Or should I say, galloped.

It was Tigress, my first horse. With Tigress in my life it didn't matter if I never went out on a date, never had a boyfriend, never got married, all distinct possibilities in my adolescent head; I had her to love and care for instead. It seemed an acceptable trade-off.

She was an unregistered Thoroughbred filly, a star-faced bay, to my young eyes ravishingly beautiful. My mother pulled together the $350 it took to buy her—a considerable sum for a green-broke, three-year-old back then. We brought her home to our ten acres in Northern California, where we'd settled after my father had retired from the Air Force.

In the beginning, I remember just standing and gazing at her as she grazed, thinking how incredible it was she belonged to me. She seemed so big, although in fact, at 15.3-hands, she was smallish for a Thoroughbred. But she felt big to ride. She was full of energy, with springing gaits and a natural forwardness. Fortunately, she was also willing to submit to my authority, tenuous as it was at the time. I'd had a few riding lessons before acquiring her, but I was mostly a self-taught equestrian. I'd read all the books—Margaret Cabell Self, George Morris, Ronnie Mutch. I knew a fair bit in theory, but little in practice. Tigress was so forgiving though, that it didn't matter. She put up with me while I figured things out.

Not that she was bomb-proof. Tigress, despite her name, was a timid soul. She was prone to shying, but of a benign sort. When something startled her—a rock outcropping she hadn't noticed before, or a torn piece of grain bag on the ground—she didn't rear, whirl or bolt. She usually didn't even suck sideways, in that classic maneuver that can unseat the unwary. Her trademark response was the four-legged splay. She'd simply sink down, her feet sliding beyond her four corners and stare at the offending object, neck rigid, then she'd snort.

At speed of course, it was different. One time, when my sisters and I were galloping through a thick stand of live oak, my stirrup iron caught a trailing vine, dragging it after us. Naturally, to Tigress this was the proverbial saber-toothed tiger, snaring her at last. She shot forward and sideways at the same time, unseating me. Then she galloped wildly in circles, neighing her alarm. Finally, she braced to a stop a few feet from where I was still sitting in the wild oat grass, laughing. Her expression seemed to say, "Are we all right?"

She always turned to me for reassurance and she taught me the meaning of the term "honest horse." I remember being puzzled when I first heard it: An honest horse? Weren't all horses honest and if not, how did they lie? I didn't yet know that there are horses that withhold their best or try to cheat you, or indicate one thing when they mean another. Not my Tigress. She never said "no" to me out of defiance, orneriness or guile. She sometimes said, "I can't," out of fear or confusion. But she never said "I won't," or "You can't make me."

In 1968, at the Potomac West School of Horsemanship, my one class was English equitation. As I was waiting for my class, I eyed the practice jumps in the warm-up arena. There was a full course of them, of various types, all around three feet high. I'd been jumping Tigress on my own at home, over humble, homemade fences. Somehow, I suddenly felt my mare could handle that warm-up course. And if she could, I could.

Without asking anyone, I took her in, picked up a canter and rode what I now remember as a perfect course of fences. I threw my heart over each jump—all the books told you to do that—and so Tigress sailed right over as well. She could be brave, in her own way, when it counted. When riding Tigress I felt a sense of freedom, power and confidence. We were masters of the universe; bold, determined, unstoppable. We could go anywhere, do anything. It was a glorious feeling for a fifteen-year-old.

Time passed. I grew up, went to college, met and married a wonderful young man. Through it all, Tigress remained mine, sometimes leased out to another, sometimes boarded in a nearby field. Finally, in 1980, my husband and I moved onto our own twenty acres, bringing Tigress with us. She continued to be my four-legged soul mate. We had grown up together and knew each other so well that I could just think canter and off she'd go, always on the correct lead. Even in her twenties, she was a magnificent ride. Tacked up, so that her swayed back didn't show, she always looked a good ten years younger than her age. I went everywhere on her, exploring new territory around my home, camping up in the mountains. In 1985, I bought another horse to prepare for the time—still a ways off, I hoped—when Tigress would be too old to ride. It was the Thoroughbred gelding Strider who first taught me the true value of equine honesty, by not having it. He was a clever bully who learned quickly how to intimidate me. As my uncertainty grew, so did his defiance, until he would toss his head and threaten to rear if I even turned him in a direction he didn't want to go. In the year that I owned him, he nearly destroyed my confidence. Then, after he was gone, Tigress built it back.

In 1989, I lost my good mare to a malady I'd never heard of. I now know about enteroliths and their causes. But then I was oblivious to the fact that one of these mineral-based stones might be growing in my horse's gut. Because she didn't colic with it early on, I learned of it only when it became large enough to kill her. The shock of her loss stunned me. I remember vividly the moment when the vet pulled away after putting her down. I walked into my house and doubled over, keening a grief sharper than I'd ever felt before. In retrospect, I think I was grieving for my lost childhood as much as for my sweet mare. Tigress had been my living, breathing link to those happy years. She had helped me to find myself; now she was gone. I was certain I'd never own a horse again. Never would I risk that kind of anguish.

But time eventually softened the edges of my grief. In the sixteen years since my mare's death, I have indeed owned other horses, eight in all, including my daughter's ponies, Diamond and Brego. Still, I've yet to find another Tigress. And I realize I may never. I still miss her, but I'm also thankful for the twenty-two years we had together. To this day, I think of her whenever I pass her resting spot on our property, near the barn. She was the embodiment of all that I love about horses— their nobility, their strength, their beauty and gentleness and their amazing generosity of spirit.

Jennifer Forsberg Meyer

Second Chances

Seize the day; put no trust in tomorrow.

Horace

Jean and Bright Cloud share a bond that goes far beyond most animal/human relationships. He is a one-woman horse with strong opinions who, on this day, won't allow himself to be caught by anyone else. After chasing him around the pasture for awhile, they give up. Minutes later, he comes to the barn on his own to find Jean, who opens the door and watches him walk to his stall at the Chester County, Pennsylvania, farm owned by her friend, Betty.

The two have an almost spiritual bond of trust and love that has enabled Jean, in just eighteen months, to train Cloud to perform at liberty all gaits, jump nearly four feet, extend, collect, halt and stand. She uses just her hand, voice and a longe whip.

That would be a solid accomplishment for most trainers. But Jean's not a professional—she is a 73-year-old, wheelchair-bound amateur. And Cloud, only her second horse, is a coming four-year-old wild Nokota who, until eighteen months before, had roamed the North Dakota plains completely unhandled.

A local group of prominent horsepeople are helping to preserve the Nokota horse, which were hunted for sport and profit by local ranchers and nearly eradicated by federal and state agencies. The breed exists only because a few bands were inadvertently fenced into a national park in the 1940s. Cloud was among a band rounded up in order to select a few individuals for a trip east.

Cloud, a blue roan, didn't suit any prospective owners, so they intended to send him back. Cloud as usual had his own idea. "Even with three cc's of acepromazine we couldn't get him back on that truck," Betty said. "I told one of the men trying to load him, 'Someone's going to get hurt, you or the horse. Just leave him'."

For decades, the Nokota horses were hunted. In the 1960s they were rounded up by helicopter, herded into canyons and slaughtered. Those who survived to pass along their genes to today's Nokotas were those best at avoiding and outwitting people. "They became very wise," Betty observes. "Cloud was typical of a wild horse from the Plains—when startled his instinct was to run. It was difficult even to lead him. To this day no one can hold him if he wants to go."

The drivers had struggled with Cloud in an effort to get him back on the truck, making the naturally suspicious horse even more fearful. By the time he found his way into a stall in Betty's barn, he wasn't even broke to lead. "He was in my barn and he was completely unhandled and wild as a March hare," she recalls.

Cloud spent three weeks in the corner of the bullpen. "I didn't do much with him other than look at him and think, *What am I going to do with him?* I saw that he had tremendous personality, that he was a horseman's horse."

"Betty saw something in him," Jean said. "She knew I needed an outlet and was thinking about a horse so she called me."

Jean had ridden as a child but hadn't owned a horse in fifteen years. She thought her riding days were over when in her mid-thirties, through her work as a clinical microbiologist, she contracted tuberculosis that affected her spine and left her unable to walk.

As a result of her own need for help, in 1984 Jean founded the internationally acclaimed Independence Dogs, Inc. Independence dogs help those whose mobility is impaired by fetching items, opening and closing doors and bringing ringing telephones. Large dogs are also used to help people with Parkinson's, MS, muscular dystrophy and other diseases keep their balance and to help them stand.

Jean and Betty met through the organization and found they shared the same ideas about training. "We use understanding and patience," Betty says. "The severest punishment we have ever used with a dog is to roll it on its back and stare in its eyes until it understands the person is dominant."

Betty is a disciple of the classical dressage training methods used by the U.S. Equestrian Team in their winning years and trains horses the way Jean trains dogs. Which is why she thought Jean and Cloud would mesh.

"The first time I saw him in his stall he turned his back to me. I opened the door and turned my back to him. When I saw him turn fifteen degrees toward me, I'd turn fifteen degrees toward him. He'd move six inches closer. I'd do the same. Within two and a half hours he had his nose pressed against my forehead," Jean recalls. Although wary of everything, Cloud was never frightened of her wheelchair. Within days, Cloud walked on a lead shank in a paddock, led by Jean, who turned her wheelchair to lead him. He was hesitant, but never fought her. "We won each other's trust, respect and love," she said.

After working with Cloud for ten months, Jean decided it was time for her to take a ride, something she'd known she'd do from the first moment she saw him trot. She had one of the boarders back him and that went well. "We constructed a ramp and I got up there with my wheelchair and each time I would get close to him he would move away, something he hadn't done with the girl. I finally realized he thought I was getting on wheelchair and all." She moved into another chair, placing the wheelchair where Cloud could see it and he stood while she mounted. "He was wonderful," Jean said of the ride. "He's not an old deadhead, either," Betty counters, "I wouldn't get on him."

The arena floor has a panel of plywood in the center, on which Jean's wheelchair rolls easily. Cloud stands with his head close to her's. She talks to him quietly and feeds him treats before releasing him from the lead. Cloud works at liberty. He trots each direction, extending and collecting at signals from Jean. He practices his latest lesson, walk/reverse/walk with no break in stride. He stops and stays at a halt, never taking his eyes from Jean while cavaletti and a ten-foot bounce are constructed. Jean sends him over the jumps again and again, as the final jump is raised several times. When Cloud pulls the top rail, he retreats to the corner, head down, pawing.

"He's very disappointed in himself, he doesn't do that unless he's upset with himself. He wants to try again. He wants to please me in the worst way," Jean said, "He's given my life a great deal of meaning. I went back to horses at age seventy-two and he put the life back in me. They give you something humans can't."

The final rail is back up and Jean sends Cloud around for another pass. This time he clears it by eighteen inches.

Stephanie Shertzer Lawson

A Procession for Kohen

*F*aith, *n. Belief without evidence in what is told*
by one who speaks, without knowledge, of things
without parallel.

Ambrose Bierce

As with most of our horse rescues, this one began with a
phone call. An ex-race horse, winning nearly a million dollars
but no longer able to breed was now considered useless by
his owner and being readied for slaughter. The call came
from an employee of the stable who had grown attached to
the horse and was hysterical at the thought of his fate. Would
we please accept him? Two weeks later, Kohen would arrive
at our facility.

I placed Kohen in isolation until the vet could examine
and geld him. The surgery was a miracle in itself as it would
prove, due to massive infection, the horse was lucky to be
alive. Life had not been easy for this big, beautiful stallion.
His legs showed signs of pin firing and he had been nerve
blocked—both legal procedures performed to permit a horse
to continue racing with injuries but without being aware of
his pain. Definitely not the miracle fix it appears to be. Kohen
could no longer feel the lower part of his legs, causing him to

walk with a stiff, robotic gait. Unable to feel a touch, in order to lift his front feet, he had to be thrown off balance. Over the years, the effect of these procedures would cause unimaginable damage to his back.

Kohen was an easygoing horse. He loved people and got along well with all the other horses. In fact, they had developed a deep-seated bond that even I wasn't aware of.

Several years had passed when one afternoon I noticed Kohen and another horse, a mare, romping and playing in the field. Fascinated by their antics, I watched them for awhile. They were having such great fun when suddenly the little mare bumped Kohen off balance and he fell. Try as he might, he was unable to get up. I ran to him and with much maneuvering and an adrenaline rush, I positioned myself under his back end and lifted him to his feet. Still struggling, he was up but I didn't know for how long. I telephoned the vet.

The vet arrived, checked Kohen thoroughly and told me that I had done everything possible. He explained that the many years of added stress on Kohen's back, due to his compensating for his front legs, had caused his spine to give out. He said the humane solution would be to euthanize Kohen.

Horses normally run from illness or death of another horse, but to our amazement as the vet prepared to release Kohen from his pain, all the other horses gathered around him. As I tried to hurry them off, they pressed tighter and tighter against Kohen, as if to embrace him. As Kohen passed away, I watched in awe as the horses very slowly and evenly parted, easing his lifeless body to the ground.

I covered him and waited for my husband to come home from work. When we returned to the field, Kohen was uncovered. Scuff marks and patches of missing hair were evidence that his devoted pasture mates had tried to wake him, to get him to rejoin the herd.

As we raised Kohen to move him to the back ridge we beheld a sight we had never seen before. Eighteen horses, one following immediately behind the next and with their noses to the ground, formed a procession and followed directly behind us to Kohen's gravesite two fields away. Total silence from all except, at the very end of the procession, our little donkey mournfully braying.

When Kohen was placed in his grave and covered, his loyal companions returned to their fields. The little donkey would cry until the chimes of midnight.

What was this special bond and why with this horse? Maybe the others realized that, other than my husband and me, Kohen had no one. After the hundreds of thousands of dollars he won and the many, many top race winners he produced, he was callously discarded. Not seen fit for anything but slaughter by anyone but one determined employee who thought he deserved more in life.

I'll never forget and probably never again see, eighteen horses and a little donkey in a proud procession to lovingly say good-bye to their forever friend.

Sissy Burggraf

5

JUST HORSIN' AROUND

Whose laughs are hearty, tho' his jests are coarse, and loves you best of all things— but his horse.

Alexander Pope

The Good Deed

Shoot for the moon. Even if you miss, you will land amongst the stars.

Jill McLemore

"Oskar is trustworthy, loyal, helpful, friendly, courteous, kind, obedient, cheerful and brave." Was the breeder talking about a three-year-old stallion or a Boy Scout? I originally called Connie, owner of Carrousel Farm, to inquire about Oskar's brother Hank, who was listed for sale on the farm Web site. Connie politely—and a little too cheerfully—informed me that Hank was no longer for sale. After he became the highest scoring horse at the biannual Lipizzan evaluation, the decision was made that he was simply too good to be sold. He was destined to become a Carrousel Farm breeding stallion and Connie's personal riding horse. No wonder Connie sounded cheerful.

For me, the news was shattering. I had been fantasizing about this horse for over a year. The majestic image of young Hank kept me going through one of the darkest and most difficult periods of my life. In 2001, my husband and I were living in Saudi Arabia. The Middle East region was destabilizing and knowing we needed to be light on our feet and prepared to move home on short notice, I sadly found new homes for my beloved horses. They could not be shipped to the United States because of a blood parasite that was common in the region but not permitted in horses imported to North America.

I continued to ride, but I felt emptiness in my heart. As a horsewoman, I knew the empty space could only be filled by a special horse—not my friend's horse, not a leased horse, but "The One" horse that was all my own. Because I had no idea when we would actually leave the Middle East, I thought it would be much easier to survive if a real live horse played the starring role in my horse fantasy. It had to be one that I could actually buy when we returned home. Among other things, it had to be incredibly smart and calm and kind. After months of painstaking research, I decided it also had to be a Lipizzan. We were fortunate to be allowed Internet access during our final year in Saudi and while surfing the Web, I found my "leading man." He was a Lipizzan, he was almost perfect and he was named Hank.

The words "Hank is no longer for sale" hit me like a well-placed kick to the chest. Choking back profound disappointment, I asked, "So, who's your second best horse?" From the description Connie gave, it sounded like Oskar was also too good to be sold. Why would anyone want to sell an excellent physical specimen of a horse whose list of personal attributes sounded like a page right out of the Boy Scout Handbook? It was post 9/11, the economy was sluggish, the horse market was down and Connie had forty-six Lipizzans to feed and more on the way. Some of them had to be sold.

My husband and I had just relocated back to the States. Our household shipment had not yet arrived, I didn't have so much as a lead rope in my possession, but something told me not to put off looking at this remarkable horse. I lost the opportunity to buy Hank, I was not about to pass up the chance to buy his brother Oskar. What if this Boy Scout actually turned out to be "The One" that would finally fill the ever-expanding emptiness of my aching horsewoman's heart?

Early April is not exactly the best time of year to go horse shopping in Oregon. We packed our rubber boots and rain ponchos and headed up from sunny California to the soggy northwest. As if to bless the occasion, the California sunshine followed us. Our journey was charmed from beginning to end.

Anyone who has had firsthand experience with Lipizzans knows that they choose their riders as much as their riders choose them. Once a Lipizzan bonds to its human, the bond is intense and it is for life. Like most Lipizzans, Oskar has an almost dog-like desire to please. His favorite sound is the snapping of carrots. But his second favorite sound is undoubtedly laughter. Oskar has figured out that cleverness leads to laughter, laughter leads to treats; the more the laughter is heard, the more treats will be forthcoming.

Early training of my beloved Boy Scout went smoothly. He proved to be a rapid and enthusiastic learner. The merit badges stacked up quickly. Like many young horses, Oskar enjoyed exploring the world with his mouth. When I was tacking him up, I noticed Oskar would pick up and hold his protective leg boots and gently put them down again. Giving a young stallion a job to do is a great way to keep him occupied and out of trouble. I decided to teach Oskar to hand me the leg boots as I needed them. Not only did Oskar willingly hand me the boots, he seemed to know the order in which to present them; bell boots first, front boots next, hind boots last. It was eerie, but convenient. Oskar was happy to participate and I was happy to decrease the frequency with which I bent over and put my head down near the hooves of a young horse.

As I was tacking up one day, a friend watched and marveled at mommy's little helper. She said, "I'll bet you could teach him to fetch a ball!" After my ride, I decided to see if my friend was right. I challenged myself to accomplish the task in three days. It took five minutes. Word of the amazing stupid pet trick spread rapidly through the barn. Oskar gave command performances frequently and with vigor. On days when the children's program was in session, the students relentlessly hurled the ball. Oskar fetched it. The children laughed and cheered him on. When the parents came to take the children home, Oskar would stand in his paddock with the ball in his mouth watching the last car go down the dusty drive and out the gate. It seemed like the horse could never get enough.

About a week after Oskar mastered the art of retrieving, the full scope of his amazing intellect was revealed. We were almost finished with our daily schooling session in the arena when I carelessly dropped my whip on the ground. I was confident in Oskar's ability to pick up the whip and hand it to me. I was not so confident in my ability to communicate to Oskar what I wanted while I was sitting on his back. I decided to try.

I rode toward the whip. Oskar's ears went forward letting me know he saw it on the approach. We halted over the whip. It was in reach, but out of his field of vision because it was directly under his chin. I let out the reins and like a good citizen, Oskar stood patiently waiting for me to dismount. I didn't. By the twirling movement of his ears, I could see that his brain wheels were turning. *The reins are long. She's not getting off. She's saying something I've heard before. What does she want?* Oskar dropped his head in thought.

"Good boy!" I cooed. Then, as if to exclaim, "Well, why didn't ya' say so!" Oskar reached down, picked up the whip, bent around and handed it to me where I was sitting. It sure was good to be home.

Amelia Gagliano

Oats in My Pocket

Things which matter most must never be at the mercy of things which matter least.

Goethe

All my best memories of growing up in Callahan County, Texas, come mingled with visions of my sidekick, a short, chubby bay horse named, imaginatively enough, Little Bay. He was named that, of course, to distinguish him from some of his other horse comrades who had such names as Big Bay and Tall Bay.

Little Bay was a Quarter Horse, about 14-hands tall. He was what my dad called an "easy keeper," meaning he always had a coat of fat on his ribs even when other horses might be getting thin. Part of that was due to Bay's gift of being part Houdini and able to work open most gate latches he ever ran across. He got into the feed barn more than once and supplemented his mostly grass diet. I realize now that it was probably only by the grace of God that Bay never foundered.

My only sibling was a brother, five years older, who was by then a teenager and old enough to work summers plowing for our great-uncle. Back then we only got one TV station in snowy black and white and my closest girlfriend lived at least ten miles away. So every summer on our remote ranch, Little Bay was my chief source of entertainment. I'm sure he lost at least a little of that fat layer because of our daily workouts.

Occasionally though, Little Bay would get a break. My mom would take one of my girlfriends and me to the town of Baird, about thirty miles away, to take advantage of two other things I considered to be essential to a young girl's summer enjoyment; a swimming pool and a library. Baird had a wonderful old combination museum/library in the basement of the courthouse. I loved the musty smell and the cool, damp feel of the place as much as I loved the alluring turquoise waters of the town swimming pool.

I would always come away from the Baird library with armloads of books, some of which imbedded other great horses indelibly into my heart. Misty of Chincoteague, Midnight, Smoky the Cow Horse, Flicka and her unruly son Thunderhead all became a permanent part of my psyche.

Those books greatly enriched my time together with Little Bay. The summer I read *Black Beauty*, I washed and curried and combed Bay to within an inch of his life. Inspired by *Smoky the Cowhorse*, we ranged far and wide on the high lonesome sections adjoining our home place, checking the cattle. The summer I read *National Velvet* I set up an elaborate series of pole jumps in the field, made of such cast off items as an old screen door. Then I added a few brush jumps and water jumps back in the pasture and we were in business. We had our own steeplechase course, just like Velvet and Pie!

Bay's chest no doubt contained a heart as big as Secretariat's, for he could never deny this little girl anything. I could walk back in the pasture and catch him with a few oats from my pocket, make an Indian-style halter out of a soft rope and ride him bareback to the house where we would saddle up for our next big adventure. Any other horse would evade me, staying just out of my reach or finally trotting off out of exasperation. Never Little Bay.

One of my favorite memories of Little Bay was the summer he became a racehorse. My dad had always cautioned my brother and me to never let a horse run toward the house, for that would make him spoiled. In other words, any time we turned for home, the horse might want to take the bit in his teeth and race back, which could be a dangerous thing. The rider always needed to be in control of the horse, not the other way around. My dad pointed out that among other dangers, it was a good way to lose a kneecap to a gatepost.

While I usually heeded my father's sage advice, in this case I had a little dilemma. I couldn't get Bay to flat-out run unless we were headed toward home. No doubt Little Bay had been chosen to be my kid horse in part because he had only three gears, those being walk, trot and lope. I could only find the fourth gear, the one I wanted in this case, by pointing Little Bay's compass toward home.

Finally, after weeks of training, the big day had arrived. Our track was a recently plowed field and our course would be a straight diagonal across the terraces toward home, culminating with the open gate that led to the home pasture. It was a clear sunny day and track conditions were excellent. Our racing colors were blue and pink; blue as in blue jeans and pink as in a once-red T-shirt. The crowd was restless and noisy and the other horses were high spirited and sleek, but none more so than Little Bay.

I took my feet out of the stirrups and snugged my knees up underneath the swells of my Western saddle, the way I thought a jockey ought to ride. I had my quirt ready, but it was really just for show. I never planned to actually hit Little Bay with it. I would just slap it against the top of my boot for dramatic effect.

At the sound of the pistol we were off to a quick start. The wind stung my eyes and Bay's flying mane was in my face as I crouched as low over his neck as my saddle horn would allow. The hooves of a thundering herd pounded in my ears, but at least we weren't eating dirt, because we led that field of horses the whole way.

Near the end of the race, though, it almost came un-wound. As we topped a terrace Bay gave a spasmodic mid-air leap to avoid an ugly black stain that sprang up beneath us on the other side. He almost lost his stirrupless rider, but I hung on and we finished the race, managing to get through the gate post finish line with my kneecaps intact. The lane to the barn gave us enough time to walk innocently home with a blanket of roses over Bay's neck, both of us enjoying the thrill of victory.

We left the roses and some of Bay's sweat at the barn, so no one would suspect we had committed the unpardonable sin of running toward home. Then we went to the house to tell my mom about the oily black puddle we had found in the field. She knew exactly what to do; she called an oil company to tell them that her daughter had discovered an oil pipeline leak on our property. In those days small planes flew the pipelines every few days, but this leak had not yet been reported.

Little Bay and I truly won the race that day. The proof came in the form of prize money in the mail a week later; a fifty-dollar check made out to me from an Abilene oil company. In 1960s dollars that was a lot of money. I couldn't wait to run out into the pasture and show Bay our winnings.

It wasn't until many years later that I realized Bay's great feat of athleticism that day perhaps saved us from serious injury or worse. He might have been short, chubby and slow, lacking the things the world thinks are essential to a good horse. But it's what's on the inside that really counts and Bay was big on the thing that mattered most—heart. He was a world-champion kid horse.

Little Bay has been in horse heaven for many years now. When I get there I plan to have oats in my pocket for the best friend a girl ever had.

Cindy Johnson Harper

Horse Laugh

Be like a sponge when it comes to each new experience. If you want to be able to express it well, you must first be able to absorb it well.

Jim Rohn

It was one of those horse days you look back on with embarrassment and laughter. One of those times you want to forget, yet can't help remembering.

At the time, my fifteen-year-old daughter, Mikkel, and I had been considering investing in a high-powered, expensive show horse. In search of the Holy Grail of Quarter Horses and to size up our competition, we had been to countless horse shows and watched with envy as confident women in bespoke clothes expertly guided beautiful, well-groomed and well-trained horses to ribbons, trophies, even the highly coveted buckles awarded in the Western pleasure category. In our hearts—and yes, our wallets, too—what wouldn't we give to get one of these saucer-sized buckles, the horse world equivalent of having your name in lights?

I had visions of myself in an ornate shiny vest with matching shirt, sausage-casing tight pants, suede chaps and the most fashionable color of full quill boots. My crowning glory would be an expensive Western hat, perfectly shaped to highlight my competition hair. I dreamed of sitting back-brace upright, yet utterly composed and, relaxed on my show horse. Trainers, riders, spectators and most important the judges would marvel at my ability to show no percep-tible movement as I cued my horse with just my legs and the Psychic Hotline (loose reins held above the base of the horse's neck via motionless hands).

The horse gods must have been yelling, "Wake up. *WAKE UP!*" because I was jolted back to my own barnyard reality. I had chosen my large palomino with an unknown history in the summer of 1997 before moving to our new horse ranch deep in the mountains of northern Idaho. I found him in the busy stockyard corrals, where he was ridden by migrant workers to herd cattle. With his golden coat aglow against a backdrop of black Angus and red Hereford cattle, it was love at first sight. Squinting with my mind's eye, I can still see him galloping around the arena as the savvy horse trader showed me what he could do. A magnificent animal that showed more moves in that corral than the contestants of *Can They Dance?*

In the movie, *Jerry Maguire*, Renee Zellweger has a line, "You had me at hello!" I felt the exact same way and never bothered to look for right or wrong leads, correct canter, a low neck, penny-pushing head or any other signs of a well-trained horse or untrained horse. I didn't even know about them at the time. It turned out I was in love for all the wrong reasons. Blissfully unaware of this, I named him Gabriel—as in the angel Gabriel—because we were all going to live happily-ever-after at Almost Heaven Ranch.

Shortly after we moved to the ranch, we heard about an open horse show in the neighboring town of Sandpoint. It was scheduled for August at the fairgrounds so we only had a couple of weeks to prepare. I was excited, nervous and hopeful all at once. Could Gabriel and I dance the dance?

In a role reversal, my young daughter was confident and I was not. Mikkel told me to train hard, be confident, do my best and that she'd be proud of me no matter what. I watched Mikkel on her horse Chex and tried to imitate the way she made his head and neck stay level with the ground. I worked on cueing Gabe with my legs and using subtle kissing and clicking sounds to encourage the required movements.

When it came time to purchase our outfits, they were just as we'd dreamed they'd be; we felt like Sargeants' catalog models. The big day was soon upon us with its dry, dusty heat. Cocksure, Mikkel signed up for five classes and I, almost collapsing with fear, reluctantly followed her lead.

Our first class was a trail class. Chex did it all quite well. Gabriel did fine until he had to cross a fake bridge made of slats of wood, about a thousandth of an inch off the ground. Gabe walked forward to the bridge, then backed away, then like an instant replay loop, went forward and back, forward and back, but never over. Eventually, we went around the bridge and finished the course.

The next class was the Western pleasure class. We were instructed to enter the ring at a jog. Mikkel and the other riders entered the ring as directed, at a slow, controlled jog. Soon it was my turn and I rode through the arena gate atop my magnificent Gabe, confident that we were at a slow jog. I could hear Mikkel's words, "Be positive! Think blue ribbons! Win belt buckles!" ringing in my head.

That was the right side of my brain talking; the left side of my brain soon acknowledged that Gabe and I were passing horse after horse after horse. Then the judge called out "Lope your horses," and on cue Gabe picked up the prescribed gait. But again, we were going faster and faster, passing all of the other horses in front of us. If looks could kill, we were probably dead a dozen times over because both horses and riders hate to be overtaken by someone who's out of control, but at the time I was oblivious.

As we passed in front of the judge, I could see the clipboard in his hands, the look of concentration and seriousness on his face. Looking back, I wonder how he kept from tossing out decorum and breaking into hysterical laughter. Not only was I circling the ring three times faster than everyone else, I was bouncing up and down as if my rear end and the saddle were playing Ping-Pong.

I did not know Gabe cross-fired when I first saw, bought and trained him. And that day at the show I never noticed the cattle just outside the riding ring that got his blood percolating like an old-time coffee pot, aggravating the cross-firing to new unbalanced heights. Gabe and I were having such a great time! Not only didn't we notice that we were out of step with the rest of the horses and riders—we thought we were better!

Finally, mercifully in retrospect, the class ended and we all lined up for the judge's decision. One by one, the lighter colored ribbons were awarded and both Mikkel on Chex, and I on Gabe, were still standing proudly, hopefully in formation. Perhaps we'd get first and second, something we'd always remember as a mother/daughter horse-loving team.

Well, half the dream came true: Mikkel did get first place. And Gabe and I? Nothing! I couldn't believe it. Hadn't we been worthy of a pictorial in *Horse & Rider* magazine?

Since that dusty August day in 1997, Mikkel and I have purchased a well-trained show horse and have ridden successfully in many AQHA shows. By reading and riding, watching videos and observing riders at major horse shows, I've learned a lot about showing horses. Along with that knowledge has come the realization of just how awful Gabe and I were that day.

Yet, I also appreciate the fact that Gabe is a sure-footed trail horse with instant overdrive if I feel like a four-feet-off-the-ground gallop. Gabe's kept his cow-horse heritage by helping with the branding time roundup at our neighbor's Angus ranch. And my big old palomino excels at hearing a whistle and racing from the distant pasture to the fence by the house for an apple, molasses cookie or a little loving.

In the end, I think I love Gabe for all the right reasons. I'm even glad Gabe's a lousy horse in competition. Whenever

Mikkel or I feel sad or have a bad day, we can just say, "Remember the day Gabe was a show horse?" and we immediately break out laughing until the tears stream down our faces. It's a very different—but equally wonderful—memory for a mother/daughter horse-loving team to share.

Teresa Becker

Easy Boot Bridge

When you come to a roadblock, take a detour.

Mary Kay Ash

Every week, back when I had a riding school, I used to take some of my working students, friends and anyone else who wanted to go on an all-day trail ride with picnic lunch.

One extremely hot, humid day, I coaxed Abby, Kara and Heather to join me. I chose a trail that we all really liked on hot steamy days, one that crossed the river several times so we could sponge the horses and stay cool ourselves as we crossed to the trails on the other side.

One such crossing was muddy on one side, the water belly deep to the horses and we had to go under a suspended snowmobile bridge that was not safe for horses to cross. Once across, it was back up a steep slippery bank on the other side. The only alternative, to go down into the river on horseback, was much too steep and scary, especially for young people.

So we crossed that ford and made it up the other side and continued on our way. We picked up a trot and I realized that my horse King was trotting funny. I looked down to discover that we had lost an easy boot; rubber boots I had been experimenting with that replace shoes. No one had seen the boot come off, but these little babies run $40 apiece, so we doubled back and retraced our steps hoping I could find it. We didn't see it anywhere along the trail. "Maybe you lost it when we crossed the river; it was pretty muddy there." offered Heather. So, back to the river we went.

I tied my horse up to a tree and told the girls, "I will be right back, watch King for me." I proceeded to carefully climb down the bank—remember I said it was steep. About a third of the way down, I lost my footing and slid all the way down the side of the hill into the river. The sound of laughter filtered down the hill as I came to rest, cold and wet and waist deep in the river. Gathering myself together and ignoring the laughter that was now echoing through the trees, I continued under the bridge and across to the muddy part of the embankment. Miraculously, I found the easy boot there on the other side of the river. I held it up and yelled, "Hurray, I found it!" My exuberant cheer was met with even heartier laughter from the girls . . . *What's up with that?*

With a tight grip on the boot, I started back through the mud, into the cold, waist-deep river. I crawled up the bank only to fall back into the water one more time. By now, all three girls were laughing hysterically and I'm dead sure I heard the horses snickering at my expense.

When I finally crested the hill; muddy, wet and a little peeved at the lack of sympathy, all I could say was, "What's wrong with you girls? What's so funny?" Abby, the only one who could stop laughing long enough to talk (and, who many years later would become my daughter-in-law) replied, "We were just wondering, why you didn't use the bridge." Gotta love those girls.

Vicki Austin

Begin with the End in Mind

I owe whatever success I have had to this power of settling down to the day's work and trying to do it to the best of one's ability and letting the future take care of itself.

Sir William Osler

I grew up on a farm/ranch combo in southern Idaho and wanted to be a veterinarian from the time I was knee-high to a dairy cow. Our two modest-sized parcels of land held dairy cows, beef cows, horses, pigs, sheep, chickens, dogs, cats and even tropical fish.

With such a mosaic of animals on the farm and an honest like (pigs and sheep) if not love (dogs, cats, horses) for them, I told everybody I wanted to be like the two veterinarians in our community, mixed-animal practitioners willing to look at anything the ark could throw at them.

In 1980 at the age of twenty-one, I achieved my calling and went to veterinary school at Washington State University in Pullman, Washington, with a heart leading me toward a mixed-animal career. Soon, student debt began to pile up and my wallet started leading me toward a possible military veterinarian career. Then I began to spend more time working with the veterinary school dean and my mentor, Dr. Leo Bustad, on the "People Pet Partnership" that matched elderly people with homeless pets. Those human-animal healthcare connections made me lean towards becoming a companion-animal practitioner. If I wasn't being career-whipsawed enough, an equine professor of mine, Dr. Rick Debowes, demonstrated an enviable blend of science and soul and made me wonder if I shouldn't look at being an equine vet.

I was a junior in veterinary school and it was Friday night. Tired of thinking, I had my mind on social-hour drinking with my classmates at a blue-collar bar called the Corner Club. This was before cell-hell, when you could hide out from people who didn't have electronic tethers to track you down and retract you back into reality via cell phone, beeper or PDA.

However, I was on emergency call for the equine barn at the vet school and a very persuasive receptionist tracked down my lifelong friend and roommate who knew where to find me at 6:00 p.m. on Friday night. The phone rang at the Corner Club and through the din, I heard Mike tell me that I needed to get to the veterinary school right away for an equine emergency. Relinquishing the remainder of my first draft beer, I headed for Pullman where there were some draft horses in trouble.

When I got there, I found out that we had a big problem on our hands. Literally. Four Belgian Draft horses, 17-hands high and each weighing about 2,100 pounds, had broken through a fence surrounding a Palouse-area grain field that was being planted and proceeded to belly up to the grain truck for an all-you-could-eat wheat buffet.

These horses were really sick with the clinical signs that make horse vets ill just by mentioning them: founder, laminitis and diarrhea.

Despite the serious condition of the horses and the high drama that surrounded them in the barn, my beloved equine professor, Dr. Debowes, kept his calm, using this as a great teaching case to educate two veterinary students about diagnosis and treatment of things we would certainly face in equine or mixed practice some day, even perhaps with our own horses.

My classmate and I had two basic jobs. Work on the front end of the horse, keeping the horses well-hydrated with IV fluids that coursed into the large neck veins, and give them oral medications for the pain of laminitis. The other job was to regularly use a large thermometer to measure the horse's temperature, looking for telltale signs of shock.

Now anyone who's worked around animals knows that to take their temperature you don't shake down the mercury in the thermometer, tell them to say "Ahhhh," and stick it under their tongue. Today, some veterinary clinics have fancy thermometers that use infrared to measure core body temperature from the ear canal, but when I was in school we did it the old-fashioned way. My classmate Shelly and I literally drew straws to determine which end was up, as it were. Luckily, I drew the front-row seat and was about to witness something that would determine my career path and be seared into my consciousness forever.

Shelly moved sequentially down the metal stocks to take the temperature of the horses. By the third horse, she had fallen into a rhythm; shake the thermometer down to settle the mercury, insert the thermometer, wait a minute, withdraw the thermometer, take a reading and record it on the individual horse's medical record that was held on a clipboard. As Shelly approached the fourth horse and leaned in to insert the thermometer, the horse suddenly coughed and the grain percolating in the horse's gastrointestinal track picked up speed—dramatically. Hearing the eruption, I peered around from the front of the horse to see Shelly backing away. Quite calmly, given the circumstances, with as much professional decorum as she could muster, Shelly carefully set down the thermometer and clipboard, looked at me thoughtfully and said, "Interested in trading ends of the horse on the next go around?"

With a great sense of humor and an even greater sense of our limitations, both Shelly and I decided on the spot to become companion-animal veterinarians. We also both became horse owners, but neither of us ever approached horses directly from the rear again.

We hire other vets to do that!

Marty Becker, D.V.M.

Auction Madness

*M*istakes are the portals of discovery.

James Joyce

We had just moved into a new split-level in Dayton in the late fifties when my husband, Witt, suddenly decided that our two children should grow up on a farm where we would raise Welsh ponies as a profitable sideline to supplement his public relations business. So we traded in our house for a fifty-acre farm, and Witt went to Maryland where he bought a young registered Welsh stallion from a breeder. Then he purchased two imported Welsh mares, one already in foal, from a breeder in Ohio. This, he announced, put us squarely in the pony business.

We would not go into Shetlands, he said, because they had just become expensive toys, while the Welsh pony was somewhat like a small version of an Arabian horse and made wonderful mounts for older children.

A year later, Witt decided that we weren't building up our herd fast enough and we needed another Welsh mare. Since business commitments were keeping him tied to his office, he suggested that I go to the annual fall Maryland Pony Breeder's sale at Timonium. There, he said, I could buy another fine Welsh mare already in foal. When I demurred, pointing out that I had never in my life bid on anything at auction, he cagily pointed out that it would be a splendid opportunity for me to visit my sister and her family in Washington, D.C. Witt said he was certain I could buy a mare in foal for $1,200 or less.

A cab dropped me off at the Timonium sale barn on a humid autumn evening to the sound of one hundred ponies nickering plaintively into the night air. Sitting high up in the bleachers where I could see and feel the throbbing, sweating mass of ponies and people below, I began to sway dizzily and I wondered whether I could last out the sale. I had planned to arrive early enough so that I could carefully examine the Welsh mares in their stalls, but the taxi had become ensnarled in traffic and I had only a few minutes to look over the ponies before the sale began. I had decided that there were only two bred mares with pedigrees that would mesh with our stallion's. I would bid on these if I could muster up the nerve.

Welsh ponies were selling like untarnished gold nuggets at a fire sale that night. It took me only a few minutes to realize that Witt had underestimated the amount I must pay to get a good Welsh mare. When one of the two mares I had spotted earlier was led into the ring, I had no more than wet my lips to enter the fray before the bidding had zoomed well over the $2,000 mark. The same thing happened when the second mare came in.

I was enormously relieved. I had been expunged from the bidding by prohibitive prices and now cut loose from my mission with impunity, I could sit back and enjoy the rest of the sale.

The relief was so great, in fact, that I became drowsy. It had been a long, heady day. The flight from Ohio early that morning and a joyful reunion with my sister and all those new children. Then the champagne cocktails at the luncheon meeting with the other Welsh breeders at a Baltimore hotel.

I was swaying dreamily to the auctioneer's sing-song, when something caught my eye and my head snapped up. A girl was running dramatically into the ring with the most dazzling pony I had ever seen, a tawny chestnut mare with enchanting yellow dapples dancing and glittering over her body. Her luxuriant mane shone blindingly white under the harsh barn lights and her tail shimmered and flowed behind her like a wedding veil. Great amber eyes that matched her dapples flashed through incredible white eyelashes. Her limbs were as fine as antique spoon silver.

All my life I have heard tales of persons who lost their heads at auctions. I had never believed them until it happened to me. I was hypnotized. My lips opened and I found myself bidding, once, twice and yet a third time. And then the bidding stopped. For a moment, the barn seemed eerily quiet and then the auctioneer banged down his gavel. The mare was mine for $1,000. My head cleared and I drew a long, gasping breath. I gazed one last time at my mare as she was being led out of the ring. She was beautiful beyond description. There was no doubt of that. There was only one thing wrong: She was a Shetland pony.

As this stunning fact washed over me, I shivered and tried to shake it off, like a dog shakes off water when he comes up the bank after swimming in the creek. I didn't have time to think about it now. I had other things to do. I followed my mare out of the barn and back to the stalls. I prevailed upon the seller to take her back home for several days until I could send a truck for her. Then I went around to the cashier's booth and wrote a check.

Back in my room long after midnight, I understandably tossed about for a way to break the news to Witt that the mare I had purchased was not a Welsh mare. But whatever I conjured up as my end of the conversation, the only reply I could ever come up with at his end was, "You bought a what?"

Wearily I picked up the telephone. I knew he was waiting for my call. May as well give it to him straight.

"I lost my head and bought a Shetland mare."

As I heard Witt's voice, it seemed to reverberate from peak to peak over the Appalachian Mountains that separated us. I held the receiver away from my ear. I really didn't need the telephone to hear him.

"YOU BOUGHT A WHAT!"

When Severn Poppet backed daintily out of a trailer and twirled around on our driveway, the children had been hanging on the fence for hours waiting for her. I had made a deal with a young neighbor who owned a horse trailer to make the trip to Baltimore to fetch her.

In the meantime, our seven- and four-year-old had worked themselves up into a frenzy of anticipation. They had always been a little frightened of our Welsh ponies, too spirited and too large for them to consider as pets, but Poppet's name alone gave them visions of a pony cut down to their size. Now, when they finally saw her, I knew she exceeded their wildest expectations. Their eyes became as round as bright coins, their hands reached out awesomely to touch her gloriously silky mane and tail, to stroke the unreal yellow dapples that seemed to ripple under her skin.

Watching their joy, I suddenly felt very guilty. I had obtained this pony on a selfish impulse, not consciously thinking of my children at all. Without realizing it, I had brought home the touchstone pony of every child's dream.

After countless trips to the barn that night for one more look at Poppet, each time returning with bigger stars in their eyes, Stoyer and Liz finally dropped into bed exhausted, undoubtedly I thought, with yellow dapples dancing in their heads. Witt went back out to the barn to turn out the lights for the last time and when he came in he reported that the children had bedded Poppet down with so much straw that she was floating in it right up to her white eyelashes.

As he reached up to put the flashlight back on the shelf, he muttered something to himself that I couldn't quite make out. It sounded like, "To heck with it. Kids that happy ought to be worth something." He never again mentioned that I had complicated our breeding program by introducing Shetlands.

At the giddy moment when I had outbid everyone in the sale barn for Poppet, I was oblivious of the premium that was riding with her. She was carrying the foal of a much beribboned Shetland stallion; I had purchased a bred mare.

At least I had done one thing right.

Carrie Young

Kids Bounce, Adults Don't!

Maturity means being emotionally and mentally healthy. It is that time when you know when to say yes, when to say no and when to say WHOOPEE!

Author Unknown

I love watching my daughter ride because she loves riding fast and jumping high. She also loves getting on her pony she outgrew several years ago, tying the reins in a knot and cantering a course bareback while holding her hands straight out to the side.

Now call me crazy, but I find having access to the reins to be an important part of riding. In fact, I can think of a lot of things I would rather do than jump without reins—mop the floor, fold the laundry, figure out my taxes, go to the dentist, put up hurricane shutters. Things I try to avoid at all costs would suddenly take precedence over riding if I knew I had to go on a rein-less ride.

I know many adult riders would look at me like my hair was on fire if they knew I no longer had the need for speed or danger. There are plenty of adult riders out there who still love the thrill of a good gallop on a lightening fast steed.

Unfortunately, I have turned into the kind of rider who wants a steed that hasn't galloped in many years and has enough sense not to come out of their stall if they spot lightning within a twenty-mile radius.

Yes, I have become a riding wimp! The older I get the more wimpy I have become, but I haven't become wimpy without reason. It is a result of my theory that the older we get the less we bounce. And when I say bounce, yes, I am referring to falling off the horse and hitting the ground. If you watch a kid fall off, they usually hit the ground, bounce to their feet in a matter of seconds, stick their hands in the air like they have just finished an Olympic gymnastic routine and proclaim, "I'm all right!"

Kids may bounce, but adults usually don't. When an adult falls off, they tend to sit on the ground for a minute and try to figure out if anything is broken. If all bones seem in order, then they try and decide what went wrong before standing back up. It makes sense to me. A quiet time to sit and reflect is sometimes necessary in our busy world. So what if it happens to be in the middle of the ring while others are waiting. And so what if it holds up a lesson, a clinic or a show. I think kids these days don't have enough patience, so learning to wait while an adult enjoys a few minutes of relaxation while sitting on the ground under their horse may just help teach kids an important quality.

I watched my adult friend Linda fall off her horse while jumping not long ago and was impressed that even though she didn't bounce, she was back on her horse in under five minutes. But at the end of her ride when she dismounted, she realized her knee had taken a nasty whack during the fall and she couldn't really walk.

Now a child rider would just hop on one leg if this happened, but for some reason adults usually do better on two legs. Maybe it's because we haven't hopped in so long we have forgotten how, or maybe it's because we know if we have to hop around the barn for the entire day we will get so tired we will eventually fall over, land on a hoofpick and end up needing stitches. And who wants to explain a strange hoofpick injury to the nurse in the emergency room.

After I left Linda nursing her hurt knee, I thought about my theory on adults not bouncing. That's when it hit me that even though I might not bounce anymore, there are areas of my life that are better because with age I have gained experience and wisdom.

The first thing I thought of was that the older I get the better I am at backing up the horse trailer by myself. In fact, I can now back up the trailer and almost make it look easy. And because I am older, I know better than to take the trailer through the drive-thru at a fast food restaurant. Sometimes horse trailers get stuck if you do this, just don't ask me how I know.

The older I get the more I realize I am in charge of my own life. So if I go to Animal Care and Control to renew my dogs' rabies tags I can adopt an old yellow lab because I know I am saving her life. I can do it because I own my own farm and can have as many dogs as I want, even if I already have too many. I don't have to try and sneak a dog into a college apartment and then realize I can never hide the fact from my landlord that I have a dog because the dog ate all the baseboards and chewed up the curtains. Don't ask me how I know this either.

The older I get the more fun I have going to watch a Grand Prix at Wellington. I can sit in the stands and not suffer from any nerves because, thankfully, I am only a spectator and not showing. Because sometimes if your nerves get too bad while showing you will hyperventilate and have to sit in the warm-up ring with a paper bag over your mouth while all the other riders stare at you. Don't ask me how I know.

And finally, the older I get the more I enjoy watching my daughter riding around the ring with no hands, jumping her pony and having fun. I know if she falls off she will probably bounce and I know that I will never in a million years try something so silly because if I did and I happened to fall off, I know adults don't bounce. Just don't ask me how I know!

Jan Westmark

The View Between My Horse's Ears

If the sight of the blue skies fills you with joy, if a blade of grass springing up in the fields has power to move you, if the simple things of nature have a message that you understand, rejoice, for your soul is alive.

Eleonora Duse

My favorite thing to do is ride. My second favorite thing is taking pictures. I always have my camera with me. Many of the pictures have my horse's ears in them, sticking up like an artist's thumbs as he lines up his view. Even though I have been snapping pictures from horseback for years, I had never really thought about the significance of those ears until recently.

I had no agenda that hot August morning. I just wanted to get out of town and go riding. I trailered out to the Wilson Creek area of the Owyhee Mountains in Southwestern Idaho. I took my little Arabian mare, Rushcreek Hollie, and my only plan was to explore some new territory around the hills and through the canyons. I was continually scanning the countryside for wildlife as we went along the narrow dirt road. Although all the creeks and drainages were dry, there were still plenty of chukkar, rabbits, lizards, an occasional rattlesnake and even wild horses. I'd never seen the horses, but I'd come across their tracks and stud piles quite often, so I knew they were there . . . somewhere.

Hollie walked along the dry creek bank and I heard the chukkar calling to each other. There were at least fifty of them and they scurried through the sagebrush as we got closer. They had been enjoying the coolness of lush green grass surrounding an old, cement water trough that must have been spring fed. The wild horses also frequented the trough. Hoof prints were all over the place. Nice, unshod hooves, narrow toes and wide heels, even a foal track. Hollie wasn't interested in water; she was busy sniffing the air, knowing she was not alone.

On impulse, we followed the tracks. The possibility of getting a glimpse of a mare and foal was really exciting. The tracks were hidden in the rocks but every now and then, I noticed one. I'd ridden at least five miles back into the canyons, far from civilization and I just kept trailing the tracks. Wondering as I studied the hillsides, if a wild horse was watching us, I whispered to Hollie, "This is just like one of those old novels I read as a kid. We're tracking wild horses!" Hollie was busy sniffing branches and undoubtedly picking up the horses' scent left behind as they rubbed the brush. We'd been following the tracks from the trough for about fifteen minutes, along the dry washes and through rocky gullies, and then the tracks veered and went up a hill. I kept scanning the country all around as we climbed up, thinking a horse could be hiding in that tall sagebrush. Just in case something might be near the top, we crested the hill slowly and cautiously, but saw nothing. Hollie started trotting again while I kept looking. She was on a mission and wanted to find those horses as much as I did.

Then, it looked like there was something in the distance, so I stopped her. It was just a big rock. So, off we went. But wait a minute; the rock swished its tail! It was a horse! Get out the camera. Then I saw another. We slowly walked closer and I could see a third horse. I'd never seen wild horses this close before. They were eating dry grass in an area with red clay soil and they blended in perfectly. I took a quick picture as Hollie walked closer. I marveled at how sleek and fat they were, such incredibly hardy horses.

Then one threw its head high in the air, on full alert, sniffing the air. A magnificent chestnut with so much presence and stature that left no doubt he was a stallion. His blazed face watched us intently for a couple of minutes, then he snorted and started toward us. I watched with complete awe as the three of them headed our way at a trot. I had ridden out alone that day and one horse and rider wasn't too intimidating to this bold stallion. I got a bit anxious and stepped off the mare so the stallion wouldn't get too close. Seeing a person standing on the ground, the stallion screeched to a stop and stared at us. Hollie's gaze was fixed on the horses. Then the trio took off at a gallop, all the while the stallion had his head turned looking at my mare as I kept snapping pictures.

After a couple hundred yards, the stallion stopped again. Three more horses came galloping up and the foal was in the middle. They were all chestnut or dark brown, nature's camouflage for the brown and red colors of the high desert landscape. The little band of six met up, paused to look at us and started to trot away. The stallion had to stop and take one last, long look at my mare, his head held high and proud. Then they were gone.

What a wonderful treat I had been given! To observe these beautiful animals, running free, was the greatest adventure I could have asked for. It certainly wasn't what I had set out to do that morning when I saddled up. I experienced a million emotions, all beyond words and I was glad I had my camera to capture the moments on film.

It was time to find our way back. Hollie picked up a trot as I turned her in the direction of the trailer. I snapped a few more pictures of a small rabbit and some fascinating rock formations. I flipped the digital camera over to look at the pictures I had taken and chuckled at the tips of Hollie's ears at the bottom of most of them. I rubbed her neck and told her how pretty her ears were. How wonderful the view is between those soft black-tipped ears! I've seen magnificent waterfalls, mountain streams sparkling from the moonlight and a variety of wildlife in many isolated places, with the focal point often being between my horse's ears. It's a blessing that I hope to experience for many years to come.

I felt very humbled and lucky to have watched the wild horses, invited by their tracks into their world. As Hollie trotted along, I thanked her for the journey that day and thanked God for the beautiful horses. These tough horses are part of our Western heritage. May they always be there for someone else to view between their horse's ears.

Karen Bumgarner

Southern Spirit

The fly cannot be driven away by getting angry at it.

African proverb

I remember spending my summers down in Woodstation, Georgia, riding my horses in a big field in front of grandmother's house. She would sit on her front porch in her rocking chair and watch me canter through the tall fescue. I rode constantly, in the heat of muggy days and into the evening to the cicadas' serenade. When it became too dark to see, I'd climb off my horse, go sit with Grandma and listen to her stories of the past.

More than once, Grandma told me that loving horses ran in our family. Some of the men in our family had ridden in the cavalry. But the story I liked best was the one about her grandmother who had lived through the Civil War.

The days and nights must have been long for Matilda Arnold Seabolt while her husband McKinley fought along with the Georgia 23rd Infantry regiment up north. A young mother in her twenties, Matilda lived with her parents in Naomi, Georgia, a small community tucked in the valley next to the long and low-slung Taylor's Ridge. She cared for her small daughter, Addie, and doted on her favorite horse, a fine gray mare she called Snip.

Matilda had heard stories about a band of irregulars called the Gatewood Scouts who terrorized the area and took whatever they could—hogs, chickens, eggs, flour and horses. In rural areas of the South, mules and horses were especially valuable because they were the only way to get around. Horses and mules also helped fight the Civil War and many died in battle or from disease.

Hearing the Gatewood Scouts were in the area and fearing for her mare's safety, Matilda hid Snip in the deep woods near Taylor's Ridge.

Soon the band of Scouts arrived at Matilda's family farm and stole bushels of potatoes and fruit, syrup, tobacco and hogs. When one of them took little Addie's red bucket, she cried. Seeing her tears, the Scout relented and gave it back. By the time they were ready to depart, the Scouts had rounded up several horses they wanted but before they left, they somehow found out about the mare in hiding. They demanded the horse be brought to them at once. When Matilda refused, they threatened to burn down her family's house. Fearing the loss of her home, she asked her father, Billy Arnold, to retrieve Snip from the woods. When he returned, the Scouts announced that they were taking the horse and heading south to Calhoun, about fifteen miles away.

To everyone's surprise, Matilda jumped up on Snip's wide back and told the soldiers she would ride the horse herself. The Scouts asked her to dismount but she refused, saying that wherever her horse went, so did she. She told them she intended to stay with the horse to ensure she was cared for properly. So off they rode, a ragtag group; the band of men and one very determined southern woman aboard her mare. They headed up Taylor's Ridge into the twilight.

Through the long night they rode, the men pleading with her to get off her horse. She wouldn't budge. The men told her they didn't want to hurt her but that she had to get off and return home. She clung on to Snip's long mane and kept up with the Scouts' pace.

By the time dawn approached, the Scouts must have realized they had never seen such a stubborn woman. Fearing that daylight would reveal them to the locals, the Scouts finally gave up and rode away, leaving Matilda behind, still aboard her mare. Her determination had paid off. She wheeled her horse around and headed home.

Later, she would mourn for her husband who was killed in the cornfield at the Battle of Antietam. And still later, she was saddened when the South lost the war. But through it all, her courage and resolve kept her beloved Snip close and safe.

I have never seen a picture of Snip but I have seen one of my great-great-grandmother. Her pretty face is full of energy and confidence. I would have liked to have known her so I could have thanked her for the legacy she left, tenacity and a spunky Southern spirit.

Janie Dempsey Watts

Therapeutic Intervention

He who laughs, . . . lasts.

Mary Poole

Standing in the manure-filled stall, with my breath curling out in frosty puffs as I pushed the manure fork, I dejectedly glanced out at the pearly gray sky. Great. More snow. Clifford, my chestnut Morgan gelding, greedily stood with his head immersed in his feed bin and rattled his grain with emphasis. "Move over," I said crossly, poking him with the fork. He obliged, lifting one foot after another, and edged against the wall without ever raising his head. It was a day that seemed overwhelming. I had just finished doing taxes and was worried about money, settling into life on my own, and I was missing Reva terribly. Reva, my German shepherd, had been my constant companion for nearly fourteen years.

She had been gone six months and there was still an aching void. She wasn't there anymore to help me carry buckets, to protect us, to keep the other dogs in line, indeed to keep Clifford in line. The timing of her death, in the midst of my divorce, seemed orchestrated to leave me feeling completely alone. I guessed I was supposed to be learning some kind of lesson, but I didn't feel any smarter. I nudged the

manure fork under another frozen lump and felt a tear sliding coldly down my cheek. Clifford swung his head toward
me, jaw working busily. His ears perked forward. He took a
step away from the bucket and reached for the fork, grab-
bing the end of it and pulling. "Let go!" I said, waving him
away. I wiped my nose on my glove and continued scoop-
ing as I morosely thought of how an animal family was a
temporary one. Clifford, I realized, was ten years old this
year. Scorch was six. Trudy was eight. Their days were num-
bered! All of them! I squeezed my eyes shut and sobbed.

When I opened my eyes, I was immediately confronted by
the white diamond adorning the end of Clifford's nose. It
was two inches from my face. "Will you stop!" I said, reaching out and pushing on his neck. He lowered his head and
began nibbling on my hand. The white diamond jumped as
his muzzle began busily working, working, working on the
fingers of my glove, feeling delicately for the loose ends and
then pulling softly. He pulled the glove completely off my
hand and moved away with it dangling from his mouth.

I stood still. "*WHAT* are you *DOING*?"

His head went up, up, up, pointing at the ceiling, with the
glove flipping gaily as his eye rolled toward me. Then with a
dramatic flip, he dropped it. "Nice!" I said. "Throw it in the
poop!" He reached down, picked it up, stepped over to me
and presented it to me. As I took it, he stepped back and
waited expectantly, with his tousled red forelock hanging in
his eyes, blowing warm breath that turned to white clouds
in the air. "You are definitely loony tunes!" But by now, I
was laughing. He returned to his grain then, his mission
accomplished. Had I really been thinking I was alone? I
must have been crazy.

Nancy Bailey

Horse Mania—
An Incurable Affliction

Every family has one or knows one—a young girl afflicted with horse mania. Symptoms to watch for:

- Her room is filled with miniature horse statues on the dresser, horse pictures on the walls and horse books on the shelves.
- She can rattle off the pedigrees and racing records of every Thoroughbred of note since Man o' War.
- She sits for hours watching reruns of *National Velvet* and *Seabiscuit.*

If you're observing any of this behavior, you have a horse maniac in your family. Boys usually are not prone to this malady, but with girls, it seems to be a nationwide epidemic. I speak with authority because I have been horse crazy since say, age one. My first words, I am told, were not "Mommy" or "Daddy," but "Oosie, Oosie." I remember constantly begging for a horse, but being a city girl, the answer always came back, "When you grow up and have your own place, you can have as many horses as you want."

Well, I grew up, married and had a nice home in the suburbs, but the passion still burned to someday have a horse of my own. My husband, bless his soul, finally said, "Let's not always be saying someday. Before we know it, time will fly by and all we can do is look back on those somedays that never happened. If we're going to do it, let's do it now."

So, we sold the house, packed our belongings and with two little boys and a dog we moved onto a ten-acre ranchette, complete with a small barn and corral. It was there I realized my lifelong dream and along the way learned some very important lessons in horse ownership that I would like to share with you today.

Rule #1. Familiarize yourself with the language of "horse-manese" so you can decipher some of those glowing terms as you search the classified ads for that special creature. For, like any other sales pitch, there may be a world of difference between what they say and what they mean. For example:

"Gentle, but spirited." You can get into the saddle before taking off at a dead run.

"Needs experienced rider." You're lucky to get one foot in the stirrup before taking off at a dead run.

"Loads well." You won't have any trouble getting this horse into your trailer, but you may find him upside down by the time you get where you are going.

"Definite show potential." Every horse ever foaled is definite "show potential" to its owner.

"In the ribbons every time shown." Shown once, placed sixth out of six.

"To good home only." Anyone with cash in hand will be found to have a good enough home.

"Twelve-year-old gelding, sound, no vices. Reason for selling, daughter has discovered boys are more fun." This ad might be the one to follow up.

Rule #2. It is impossible to own just one horse. You will soon discover you want one for your husband so he can join you on trail rides, plus ponies for the boys until they are old enough to have a horse of their own. However, by that time, they probably have figured out that horses are synonymous with work and they would rather play baseball.

Rule #3. If you have a mare, an unwritten rule dictates that you will have a foal—and then another and another. You justify this passion by stating you will sell those foals and turn this whole thing into a money-making venture. But if you thought you had crying spells when you wanted a horse so badly, it is nothing compared to what will happen when it is time to sell one of those babies.

Rule #4. With your ever-increasing band of horses, you will find you need to enlarge that small barn behind the house and your horses will spend their time idly watching as you spend your time building barn additions and more fencing. Endless discussions with your spouse will follow about whether to put a second mortgage on the house for the Kentucky-style, white-rail fencing you want, or pay attention to the pocketbook and settle for the much cheaper barbed wire.

Which leads to **Rule #5**. The propensity to get themselves hurt in a barbed wire fence is directionally proportional to the cost of the horse. Your "for fun" family-types might manage to stay sound (horseman's word for healthy), but your newly acquired, registered show horse will invariably get himself caught in the barbed wire. The series of vet calls, medication, shots and a whole summer of unridability can make barbed wire one of the most expensive forms of fencing you can put up. Like a horseman friend of mine told me, "Horses and 'bob-wire' don't mix. Cattle, yes—horses, no."

Rule #6. If you have a horse, eventually you will want to show that horse. From past experience, I put owning a show horse on a par with the IRS in getting rid of any extra money you might have lying around—rather like pouring your life savings down a black hole. The purchase of the horse is nothing compared to the numerous and very expensive equipment you suddenly need in order to get into the show ring. But, like the rest of us horse maniacs, when you come out of the class with a ribbon clutched in your fist, you'll be the first in line to empty your pockets for the next show.

After reading this, if you still decide to go ahead with the adventure, let me be the first to welcome you to this wacky, wonderful, upside-down world where success is measured in strips of colored ribbons and the show ring becomes the center of the universe around which everything else revolves. And when you find yourself sleeping in the barn, waiting for your favorite mare to give birth to her first foal and you hear those never-to-be-forgotten sounds of new life rustling in the straw, you will admit, yes, you are a horse maniac; yes, it is incurable and yes, you wouldn't trade it for anything else in the world.

Jacklyn Lee Lindstrom

More Chicken Soup?

We would love to hear your reactions to the stories in this book. Please let us know what your favorite stories were and how they affected you.

Many of the stories and poems you have read in this book were submitted by readers like you who had read earlier Chicken Soup for the Soul books. We publish at least five or six Chicken Soup for the Soul books every year. We invite you to contribute a story to one of these future volumes.

Stories may be up to 1,200 words and must uplift or inspire. You may submit an original piece, something you have read or your favorite quotation on your refrigerator door.

To obtain a copy of our submission guidelines and a listing of upcoming Chicken Soup books, please write, fax or check our Web sites. Please send your submissions to:

Chicken Soup for the Soul
P.O. Box 30880
Santa Barbara, CA 93130
fax: 805-563-2945
Web site: *www.chickensoup.com*

Just send a copy of your stories and other pieces to the above address. We will be sure that both you and the author are credited for your submission.

For information about speaking engagements, other books, audiotapes, workshops and training programs, please contact any of our authors directly.

A Helping Hand

A portion of the proceeds from the sale of each copy of *Chicken Soup for the Horse Lover's Soul II* will be donated to the Thoroughbred Charities of America. TCA is the largest umbrella non-profit organization of the Thoroughbred industry. TCA's sole mission is to raise money for distribution to over 150 organizations involved with Thoroughbred rescue, retirement, rehabilitation, research, education, backstretch and therapeutic riding programs. TCA differs significantly from most fund-raising organizations by one huge factor. With the exception of one paid employee, TCA is administered entirely by unpaid volunteers. This allows TCA to grant over 93 cents of every $1 raised each year. The TCA Board of Directors consists of some of the most knowledgeable and respected people in the Thoroughbred industry and they are very proactive in TCA fund raising and grant giving activities. TCA has issued over $12 million in grants in 15 years to more than 150 organizations in 34 states with the support of the Thoroughbred industry.

Thoroughbred Charities of America (TCA)
P.O. Box 3856, Midway, Kentucky 40347
(859) 312-5531 *www.thoroughbredcharities.org*

Get More Connected to Horses. AQHA Can Help.

AQHA's free 4aHORSE referral service is your one-stop source to locate professional trainers, breeders and riding instructors and to further your equine education. AQHA has several programs and offers real options for the horse-loving public, especially the casual horse lover. The American Quarter Horse Association is ready to help you discover how special horses can be.

American Quarter Horse Association (AQHA)
P.O. Box 200, Amarillo, TX 79168
(806) 376-4811 *www.aqha.com*
1 (877) 4-A-HORSE *www.4ahorse.com*

Who Is Jack Canfield?

Jack Canfield is one of America's leading experts in the development of human potential and personal effectiveness. He is both a dynamic, entertaining speaker and a highly sought-after trainer. Jack has a wonderful ability to inform and inspire audiences toward increased levels of self-esteem and peak performance. Jack most recently released a book for success entitled *The Success Principles: How to Get from Where You Are to Where You Want to Be*.

He is the author and narrator of several bestselling audio- and videocassette programs, including *Self-Esteem and Peak Performance, How to Build High Self-Esteem, Self-Esteem in the Classroom* and *Chicken Soup for the Soul—Live*. He is regularly seen on television shows such as *Good Morning America, 20/20* and *NBC Nightly News*. Jack has co-authored numerous books, including the *Chicken Soup for the Soul* series, *Dare to Win* and *The Aladdin Factor* (all with Mark Victor Hansen), *100 Ways to Build Self-Concept in the Classroom* (with Harold C. Wells), *Heart at Work* (with Jacqueline Miller), and *The Power of Focus* (with Les Hewitt and Mark Victor Hansen).

Jack is a regularly featured speaker for professional associations, school districts, government agencies, churches, hospitals, sales organizations and corporations. His clients have included the American Dental Association, the American Management Association, AT&T, Campbell's Soup, Clairol, Domino's Pizza, GE, Hartford Insurance, ITT, Johnson & Johnson, the Million Dollar Roundtable, NCR, New England Telephone, Re/Max, Scott Paper, TRW and Virgin Records. Jack has taught on the faculty of Income Builders International, a school for entrepreneurs.

Jack conducts an annual seven-day training called Breakthrough to Success. It attracts entrepreneurs, educators, counselors, parenting trainers, corporate trainers, professsional speakers, ministers and others interested in improving their lives and the lives of others.

For free gifts from Jack and information on all his material and availability go to:

www.jackcanfield.com
Self-Esteem Seminars
P.O. Box 30880
Santa Barbara, CA 93130
phone: 805-563-2935 • fax: 805-563-2945

Who Is Mark Victor Hansen?

In the area of human potential, no one is more respected than Mark Victor Hansen. For more than thirty years, Mark has focused solely on helping people from all walks of life reshape their personal vision of what's possible. His powerful messages of possibility, opportunity and action have created powerful change in thousands of organizations and millions of individuals worldwide.

He is a sought-after keynote speaker, bestselling author and marketing maven. Mark's credentials include a lifetime of entrepreneurial success and an extensive academic background. He is a prolific writer with many bestselling books such as *The One Minute Millionaire, The Power of Focus, The Aladdin Factor* and *Dare to Win,* in addition to the *Chicken Soup for the Soul* series. Mark has made a profound influence through his library of audios, videos and articles in the areas of big thinking, sales achievement, wealth building, publishing success, and personal and professional development.

Mark is also the founder of MEGA Seminar Series. MEGA Book Marketing University and Building Your MEGA Speaking Empire are annual conferences where Mark coaches and teaches new and aspiring authors, speakers and experts on building lucrative publishing and speaking careers. Other MEGA events include MEGA Marketing Magic and My MEGA Life. He has appeared on television (*Oprah, CNN* and *The Today Show*), in print (*Time, U.S. News & World Report, USA Today, New York Times* and *Entrepreneur*) and on countless radio interviews, assuring our planet's people that, "You can easily create the life you deserve."

As a philanthropist and humanitarian, Mark works tirelessly for organizations such as Habitat for Humanity, American Red Cross, March of Dimes, Childhelp USA and many others. He is the recipient of numerous awards that honor his entrepreneurial spirit, philanthropic heart and business acumen. He is a lifetime member of the Horatio Alger Association of Distinguished Americans, an organization that honored Mark with the prestigious Horatio Alger Award for his extraordinary life achievements.

Mark Victor Hansen & Associates, Inc.
P.O. Box 7665 • Newport Beach, CA 92658
phone: 949-764-2640 • fax: 949-722-6912
Visit Mark online at: *www.markvictorhansen.com*

Who Are the Coauthors?

Dr. Marty Becker is passionate about his work fostering the special life-enhancing relationship between animals and people we call, "The Bond." Marty coauthored, *Chicken Soup for the Dog Lover's Soul, Chicken Soup for the Cat Lover's Soul, Chicken Soup for the Horse Lover's Soul* (1st edition), and *The Healing Power Of Pets,* which was awarded a prestigious silver award in the National Health Information Awards for 2002. Dr. Becker is the popular veterinary contributor to ABC-TV's, *Good Morning America,* writes a weekly Knight Ridder Tribune pet column that is distributed to over 500 newspapers, and hosts a nationally syndicated radio program, *Top Vets Talk Pets.*

An adjunct professor at both his alma mater, Washington State University College of Veterinary Medicine and Colorado State University College of Veterinary Medicine, Dr. Becker has been featured on *ABC, NBC, CBS, CNN, PBS, BBC, Unsolved Mysteries* and in *USA Today, USA Weekend, The New York Times, The New York Daily News, Washington Post, Reader's Digest, Forbes, Better Homes & Gardens, Prevention, Christian Science Monitor, Woman's Day, Woman's World, National Geographic Kids, National Geographic Traveler, Cosmopolitan, Glamour, Parents, Shape, Star, Men's Health, US Weekly, National Inquirer,* and *Cooking Light.*

Teresa Becker was born and raised in Bonners Ferry, Idaho, and enjoyed an idyllic childhood riding horses at every opportunity. A school teacher by profession, Teresa received her master's degree in sports administration and taught in elementary schools in Twin Falls, Idaho, for many years. As an adult, Teresa rode Western pleasure in Quarter Horse shows, but now her ideal day involves trail riding her palomino, Gabriel.

Marty and Teresa enjoy life in Northern Idaho and share Almost Heaven Ranch with their children, Mikkel and Lex; two dogs; six barn cats and four Quarter Horses; Gabriel, Glo Lopin, Pegasus and Sugar Babe.

Marty and Teresa Becker
P.O. Box 2775
Twin Falls, ID 83303
Phone: 208-734-8174 Fax: 208-733-5405
Web site: *www.drmartybecker.com*

Peter Vegso arrived in South Florida from Canada and founded the publishing company Health Communications, Inc. in 1976. HCI's first New York Times bestseller, *Adult Children of Alcoholics* (Woititz), appeared on the list in 1985 and has been followed by dozens more self-help and inspirational titles, including *Healing the Shame That Binds You* (Bradshaw), *A Child Called It* and *The Lost Boy* (Pelzer) and many titles in the *Chicken Soup for the Soul* series. Recognized twice by *Publishers Weekly* as the #1 Self-Help Publisher, HCI is guided in their publishing program by their mission statement, "Making a difference in the lives of our readers and the people they come in contact with."

Peter's other business interests include a professional publishing and conference company that provides training, licensing and certification for members of the mental health community, a custom design and architectural elements manufacturer, and real estate development.

Peter enjoys his 140-acre farm in Ocala, Florida, where he continues to expand his successful Thoroughbred breeding and training facility. Daily operations are handled by the hardest working manager in the world, Chuck Patton, who shares Peter's intention to not only win the Kentucky Derby but also the Triple Crown before their spirits leave this planet.

Peter Vegso
Health Communications, Inc.
3201 SW 15th Street
Deerfield Beach, FL 33442
Phone: 954-360-0909• Fax: 954-360-0034
Web site: *www.hcibooks.com*

Theresa Peluso joined the publishing enterprise of Health Communications in 1981 and was introduced to horses through Peter Vegso's interest in Thoroughbreds. Prior to that, her only connection was her Irish grandmother who loved the ponies and jumped at the chance to move to Florida in the early 1960s to be near Hialeah Park. Theresa is the coauthor of *Chicken Soup for the Horse Lover's Soul* (1st edition), *Chicken Soup for the Recovering Soul* and *Chicken Soup for the Recovering Soul Daily Inspirations*.

Theresa Peluso
Health Communications, Inc.
3201 SW 15th Street
Deerfield Beach, FL 33442
E-mail: *teri@horseloverssoul.com*

Contributors

The stories in this book are original pieces or taken from previously published sources, such as books, magazines and newspapers. If you would like to contact any of the contributors for information about their writing or would like to invite them to speak in your community, look for their contact information included in their biography.

Carrol Abel is known for her photography of wild horses and can often be found walking the desert landscape just east of Reno, Nevada. Through countless hours of observing and documenting their quest for survival, Carol has brought us the *Wild Spirit Collection*. Visit *www.wildspiritcollection.com*.

Vicki Austin lives with her husband, Ron, in Hartford, Maine. They have three sons, three daughters-in-law and three grandchildren with more on the way. She has taught riding and trained horses for thirty five years. Vicki has shown in dressage, eventing and now mostly rides long distance. Her "regular job" is as a child care aid and she also sews.

Nancy Bailey is the author of *Clifford of Drummond Island*, the true story of her rascally Morgan horse, and its sequel, *Return to Manitou*. This wildlife artist and freelance writer is originally from Michigan's beautiful Upper Peninsula. She has lived in Alaska, Arizona, California and Colorado. She now resides in Michigan with her horses, dogs and cats.

Mikkel Becker is a broadcast journalism major at Washington State University. Living summers on her north Idaho horse ranch, she is also a contributing writer for *Cat Fancy Magazine* and *Knight Ridder* newspapers.

Karen Bumgarner is a second-generation horseperson who has ridden over 19,000 miles on AERC sanctioned rides, an accomplishment shared with less than twenty other AERC members. *Western Horseman* first published her articles in 1981. As a writer, she has written over one hundred articles on endurance riding and horse care, plus two books, *America's Long Distance Challenge* and *The Endurance Horse Daily Planner* log book and journal.

Sissy Burggraf's work is also featured in the first edition of *Chicken Soup for the Horse Lover's Soul*. Sissy was born in a small town in southern Ohio. After working for eight years as a veterinary assistant, she opened Lost Acres Horse Rescue and Rehabilitation. LAHRR was established in 1994 as an alternative to euthanasia, slaughter or abandonment for abused, neglected or injured horses. Visit LAHRR at *www.geocities.com/sblahrr*.

Heidi Bylsma and her family moved to the country three years ago to fulfill her lifelong dream of having horses in the backyard. Spending most daylight hours homeschooling Daniel and his sister, Michaela, horses consume any remaining waking moments in Heidi's day. Visit Heidi on the Internet at *http://bylsma.spiritofequuus.com*

Renee Chambers is a dancer, drummer, skydiver, marathon runner and yogi. She lives on her northern Nevada ranch with her husband, Robert, and her artist-horse, Cholla. To contact Renee or enjoy Cholla's art, please visit *www.ArtistisaHorse.com*.

Cheryl Ann Dudley lives in Moscow, Idaho, and is a freelance writer and a writer for the *Appaloosa Journal*. Her published works include biographies in Harvard University's *African American National Biographies* as well as *Gale's Contemporary Black Biographies*, monthly newsletters for the Department of Health and Welfare and several poems in various journals.

Melissa Dymock has been published in the *Utah Statesman* and *The Hard News Café*. She graduated from Utah State University with a degree in journalism and a minor in animal science. Melissa was raised on a farm in Utah but is currently a displaced country girl saving for some land and a horse.

Therese Evans is a full-time assistant trainer and instructor at Wilde Fields Farm in Hunting Valley, Ohio. She lives with her husband and son in Mentor, Ohio, and enjoys eventing her off-the-track Thoroughbred, Heartland Hero. Therese has previously been published in *Reflections* magazine and enjoys writing about her love of horses as a hobby.

Amelia Gagliano lives with her husband, Gary, in Vacaville, California. Oskar continues to amaze and amuse. He has appeared in the *Horse of Kings Magazine* annual calendar, *Horse Illustrated* and *California Riding Magazine*. For photos of Oskar and more information about Lipizzans, please visit *www. carrouselfarm.com*.

Alison Gieschen has been a vaulting coach for thirteen years. The sport has truly been a transformational experience. It has developed shy and introspective kids into creative and outgoing leaders and it has taught Alison that there is sometimes a greater learning experience in being a teacher than in being a student.

Fred Glueckstein is a writer living in Maryland. He specializes in nonfiction. Fred's work has appeared in *The Chronicle of the Horse, Horses in Art, Equestrian, Mid-Atlantic Thoroughbred* and *Finest Hour*, the official journal of the Churchill Centre. He is the author of *The '27 Yankees*, (Xlibris 1-888-795-4274).

Dr. Jeanna Godfrey graduated from Texas A&M University Veterinary College in 1980. She has been in practice for over twenty five years and lives in South Texas with her husband, Larry. She is the author of the book, *How Horses Learn, Equine Psychology Applied to Training*, available through major Internet booksellers or at *www.backinprint.com*.

Barbara S. Greenstreet is a freelance writer and parenting consultant in Washington State. She and her husband, with their three children, have cared for and shared a home with a menagerie of animals from honeybees to horses. Visit Barbara at *www.barbaragreenstreet.com*.

Evelyn B. Hanggi, M.S., Ph.D., is an equine behaviorist and cognition researcher as well as the president and, along with program director Jerry Ingersoll, the cofounder of the Equine Research Foundation located in the coastal hills of Aptos, California. She is also a horse trainer, horsemanship instructor and writer for journals and magazines worldwide. Visit the ERF Web site: *www.equineresearch.org* or call (831) 662-9577.

Cindy Johnson Harper's latest project is a series of inspirational contemporary novels set in the "Big Country" region of west Texas. The series draws upon Cindy's upbringing on her family's 100-year-old ranch to portray realistic rural Texas characters and situations.

Lori Hein writes on a range of topics and publishes a travel blog enjoyed by readers worldwide, *www.LoriHein.com*. A globetrotter for twenty five years, her essay is from *Ribbons of Highway: A Mother-Child Journey Across America*, a book about family, freedom, hope and discovery that recounts Lori's 12,000-mile, back-road odyssey.

Dawn Hill is a former Pony Club leader, horse lover and freelance writer who lives in Camas, Washington. When not riding or writing, Dawn works at the Fort Vancouver Regional Library in Vancouver, Washington. Visit her Web site at *www.raincountryranch.com*.

Kathleen Hooks was diagnosed with MS when she was nineteen and subsequently changed her dreams of becoming a famous equestrian to become a high school teacher and writer in Baltimore. She recently completed a manuscript of nonfiction stories entitled, *But I Don't Want Wheelchair Grease on My Wedding Dress*. Enjoy Kathleen's writing at *www.katehooks.blogspot.com*.

Linda K. Hren received her first pony as a Christmas gift when she was eight years old. To celebrate horses as partners in healing, Linda cofounded Horses of Hope, which hosts free equine-related events for survivors of life-threatening illness and holds fundraisers for equine rescue and therapeutic riding. For information on Horses of Hope, e-mail *horsesofhope@ixpres.com*.

Anne Hope worked for over fifteen years in the operating room of a large university veterinary hospital. Anne and her husband live in Pennsylvania. They have two grown children. Anne spends most of her free time training and showing her two Welsh Corgis in dog agility.

Stephanie Shertzer Lawson is one of the lucky girls whose parents actually bought her that pony. A former American Saddlebred exhibitor and current polo player, she founded and publishes the award-winning magazine *Pennsylvania Equestrian* (*www.pennsylvaniaequestrian.com*). She also handles public relations and marketing for equestrian events including the Pennsylvania National Horse Show.

Jacklyn Lee Lindstrom, a frequent contributor to the *Chicken Soup for the Soul* series, realized a lifelong dream when she moved to the country and spent the next twenty five years raising horses. Now a golden-ager, she finds the bones too brittle, so she spends her time painting and writing about those magnificent creatures.

Vikki Marshall is the owner of Destiny Farms Sporthorses, a small breeder of Thoroughbred performance horses. She has successfully competed in hunter and dressage competitions, breeds and trains all of her own horses and prides herself on successfully re-training horses who have been neglected. She was an honorable mention in the 2002 Olympiad of the Arts short story competition and was published in *Chicken Soup for the Horse Lover's Soul* (1st edition).

Tom Maupin's work appeared in the first edition of *Chicken Soup for the Horse Lover's Soul*. He penned his contribution to the second edition while working to restore power to Hurricane Katrina and Rita victims. Tom was introduced to the wonderful world of horses by his wife, Crystal. They enjoy trail riding with their children, Jim and Stacy, as often as they can.

Cooky McClung has written equestrian features for *The Chronicle of the Horse, Practical Horseman* and other equine publications for more than thirty years. Recently retired after ten years as a staff writer for *The Kent News* on Maryland's Eastern Shore, her husband, Jim, seven children and spouses, and ten grandchildren provide endless stories about lives blessed with horses.

Merri Melde is an award-winning writer and equine photographer, an addicted world traveler, an obsessed endurance rider and the proud owner of Stormy. She is currently at work on a book of her horseback adventures around the world. You can visit Merri and enjoy her photography at *www.horseproductionsbymer.com*.

Jennifer Forsberg Meyer lives in a rural area of Northern California with her husband and their Pony Clubber daughter, Sophie Elene. An award-winning journalist and author, Jennifer writes a monthly column for *Horse & Rider* magazine and is the author of two books. She also writes and edits *Growing Up With Horses: Parents' Handbook & Resource Guide*, an annual publication.

Jane Middelton-Moz is a bestselling author and highly regarded clinician specializing in childhood trauma, suicide prevention and community intervention. Her latest book, *Bullies*, has been widely praised as an essential resource for schools and parents. Jane is the director of the Middelton-Moz Institute, a division of the Institute of Professional Practice. Contact her at *jmoz@ippi.org*.

Kim Morton is an attorney in private practice and lives in Montana with her husband and equine companions. Kim is reaching out to parents dealing with Selective Mutism in hopes she can offer insight that makes life easier for them and their children.

Wendy Wade Morton, D.V.M. and her husband, W. Bryant Morton, another veterinarian, opened Elizabethtown Veterinary Hospital in rural southeastern North Carolina in 1996. Together they raise colorful, gaited horses and hope to enjoy an early retirement at their farm in middle Tennessee to raise their boys, horses and wine grapes!

Kathryn Navarra is a freelance writer for a number of equine publications, as well as a few local business journals. Most recently, she has been working for *Unbridled TV* on a part-time basis. She has been involved with horses for the past eighteen years as an owner and rider. Kathryn's father continues his work with a local charity group to host an annual "Cowboy-Roundup" dinner with proceeds going to benefit children with cancer and their families.

Sandra Newell lives in Grass Valley, California, with her husband, Pete, and their twenty-month-old son, Christopher. Sandra has loved horses for as long as she can remember. Kahluah is retired and she is teaching Christopher how to ride.

Leslie A. Paradise learned about Horses Help, a therapeutic riding program for people with special needs, when her husband, John, suddenly passed away. Leslie joined as a volunteer and went on to become a therapeutic riding and driving instructor through NARHA (North American Riding for the Handicapped Association). She has been teaching for six years and owns two horses. Visit Horses Help at *www.horseshelp.org*.

Mark Parisi's "off the mark" comic panel has been syndicated since 1987 and is distributed by United Media. Mark's humor also graces greeting cards, T-shirts, calendars, magazines, newsletters and books. Please vist his Web site at: *www.offthemark.com*. Lynn is his wife, and business partner, and their daughter, Jenny, contributes with inspiration, (as do three cats).

Boots Reynolds is a talented, rich, good lookin' cowboy. He's a great dancer, has most of his own teeth and will have the rest paid off when he receives his check for the illustration featured in this edition. Considered a great catch, he has five wives (in his dreams) and a waiting list, will fish with just about anyone and has never told a fib... okay, maybe just one. Visit Boots and enjoy his work at *www.BootsReynolds.com* or *www.WesternClassics.com*.

Katie Reynolds lives in Denver, Colorado, with her horse, Sam. She has a degree in equine science and works for a major horse breed association.

Lawrence Schimel (New York, 1971) is a full-time, freelance author, anthologist and translator. He has lived in Spain since January 1999 where he writes picture books in Spanish, together with the Spanish illustrator Sara Rojo Pérez, such as *La aventura de Cecilia y el dragón, No hay nada como el original,* or *Como librarse de un unicornio*.

Tracy Schumer is a fourth generation native of Florida whose family roots rest in the cattle and citrus industries. Tracy takes pride in the name "Cracker." A freelance writer, photographer, and lifetime horsewoman, her work has appeared in numerous publications including *The NRHA Reiner, AQHA Journal,* and *Western Horseman*.

Valerie K. Shull has recently turned her lifelong experience, love and admiration for horses into a business specializing in products for horses at play or leisure. Her very playful Morgan horse, Zita, is the inspiration for her product ideas and her writing. Valerie lives in Ohio, but her Horseplay Products can be seen at *www.horseplayproducts.com*.

Joyce Stark lives in northeast Scotland and works for the Community Mental Health. Her hobby is writing about people around her and those she meets on her travels in the USA. She has completed a series to introduce very young children to a second language and is currently working on a travel journal of her trips, *Small Town/Big City America*. E-mail: *joric.stark@virgin.net*.

Janet Steinberg is a writer of profiles of adult, amateur riders and athletes in publications such as *Eventing, Practical Horseman, Runner's World* and various newspapers. Selected profiles have been published in a book entitled *Mining for Gold*. Her poetry appears in a coffee table photography book, *Telluride, Landscapes and Dreams*. Janet is currently working on a short story collection entitled *Step Stories*.

Jean Stewart is a writer and editor in Mission Viejo, California, who specializes in history, travel and parenting. Married for forty five years, mother of two horse-loving daughters and grandmother of one, she's been published in the *Chicken Soup* series, *Cup of Comfort, ByLine, California Living, Aviation Lifestyles* and several other publications.

Lauren Thoma is thirteen years old and has been writing since she could hold a pencil. She hopes to be a journalist someday. Lauren believes that when she looks into the eyes of her beloved new horse, Citi Lights, she sees a little bit of Bailey, "The Wonder Pony" looking back.

Tracy Van Buskirk lives in Connecticut and shares her household with her husband, two charming teenagers and an assortment of snakes, frogs, cats and dogs. Tracy is a banker, clay artist and lover of the outdoors. Her perfect day is riding in a nearby forest with friends and chatting about life.

Eileen Watkins is a freelance writer who has published articles in the magazines *Dressage Today, Horse Illustrated, HorsePeople* and *Horse Show* and she is the author of the mystery novel *Ride a Dancing Horse*, from Amber Quill Press. Eileen is collaborating with Beverlee Dee on a book about Bright Futures Farm.

Janie Dempsey Watts spent much of her childhood with horses on her family's Ringgold, Georgia, farm. Her essays have been published in *Chicken Soup for Horse Lover's Soul* (1st edition), at *www.boomerwomenspeak.com* and in *Georgia Backroads* (Fall, 2006). She also writes short stories and is at work on her second novel.

Jan Westmark writes a monthly humor column for *Sidelines Magazine*, published out of Wellington, Florida. Having spent all of her life riding, Jan runs a small lesson and show barn in Wellington. When not teaching or caring for horses, Jan puts her journalism degree to use by writing for several magazines. She also serves as a groom for her daughter who competes jumpers.

Janice Willard, D.V.M., M.S. is married with two children and lives on a small farm in Idaho shared by horses, goats, sheep and llamas. The household also includes several dogs, cats and a very officious parrot. Janice and her husband are veterinarians and Janice studies animal behavior, is passionate about music and loves to sing. Contact Janice at *janwill@turbonet.com*.

Jennifer Williams, Ph.D. is president of Bluebonnet Equine Humane Society *(www.bluebonnetequine.org)* and writes equine behavior articles for *EQUUS*. She also maintains an equine behavior Web site at *www.equinebehavior.net*. You can reach the HELP Center at *www.helpofaustin.org*.

Katrina Wood is a frequent contributing writer for equine newspapers and magazines. She specializes in long and short term equine care, breeding and foaling, injury rehabilitation and is certified in a host of alternative equine therapies. Katrina was appointed an American Morgan Horse Association Woman of the Year and received the RW Breeder's Award from the American Saddlebred Horse Association in 2004.

Carrie Young is the author of four books. She and her family had many adventures in raising Welsh (and some Shetland) ponies for forty years on their Ohio farm as told in *Green Broke,* winner of the Ohioana Library Award.

Her other books, *Nothing to Do but Stay* (a memoir), *The Wedding Dress: Stories from the Dakota Plains* and *Prairie Cooks* (written with her daughter Felicia) all feature the North Dakota background of her childhood. Contact: Univ. of Iowa Press, the Kuhl House, Iowa City, IA 52242

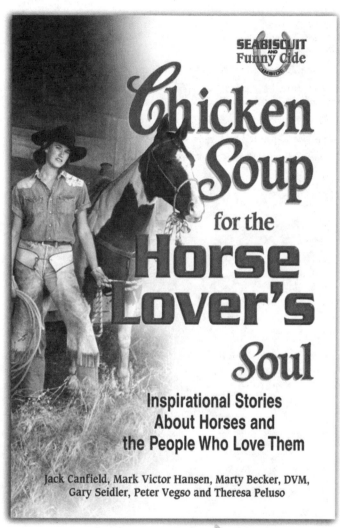

SEABISCUIT AND Funny Cide INSIDE

Chicken Soup

for the

Horse Lover's Soul

Inspirational Stories About Horses and the People Who Love Them

Jack Canfield, Mark Victor Hansen, Marty Becker, DVM,
Gary Seidler, Peter Vegso and Theresa Peluso

Code #0987 • trade paper • $12.95

Chicken Soup for the Cat Lover's Soul

Stories of Feline Affection, Mystery and Charm

Jack Canfield, Mark Victor Hansen
Marty Becker, D.V.M., Carol Kline and Amy D. Shojai

Code #3323 • trade paper • $12.95